STUDIES IN THE BRITISH ECONOMY

THE UNITED KINGDOM ECONOMY

GW00724834

STUDIES IN THE BRITISH ECONOMY

General Editor: Derek Lee

Core book: *The United Kingdom Economy* by The National Institute of Economic and Social Research

STUDIES IN THE BRITISH ECONOMY

The United Kingdom Economy

The National Institute of Economic and Social Research
London

Contributors:

F. T. Blackaby
A. J. Brown
L. F. Campbell-Boross
A. J. H. Dean
K. Jones
R. L. Major
A. D. Morgan
S. A. B. Page
R. W. R. Price
D. Savage
C. H. Thomson
M. A. Utton
G. D. N. Worswick

Published on behalf of the Commission of the
European Communities by
HEINEMANN EDUCATIONAL BOOKS

Heinemann Educational Books Ltd
22 Bedford Square, London WC1B 3HH

LONDON EDINBURGH MELBOURNE AUCKLAND
HONG KONG SINGAPORE KUALA LUMPUR NEW DELHI
IBADAN NAIROBI JOHANNESBURG
EXETER (NH) KINGSTON PORT OF SPAIN

British Library C.I.P. Data
National Institute of Economic and Social Research
The United Kingdom economy. - 4th ed. -
(Studies in the British economy).
1. Great Britain - Economic conditions - 1945-
I. Title
330.9'41'0857   HC256.6

ISBN 0 435 84581 0

Typeset by The Castlefield Press of High Wycombe
in 10/11pt Press Roman, and Printed in Great Britain by
Biddles Ltd, Guildford, Surrey

CONTENTS

Chapter 5
FINANCIAL INSTITUTIONS AND MONETARY POLICY

Chapter 6 EXTERNAL TRADE AND PAYMENTS

Chapter 7
THE MANAGEMENT OF THE BRITISH ECONOMY

Bibliographic Note

The National Institute has lately published *British Economic Policy 1960-74*, edited by F.T. Blackaby, Cambridge University Press, 1978. This study contains among other things a detailed historical account of the developments of the British economy in recent years. It also includes an extensive bibliography.

TABLES

FIGURE

PREFACE TO THE FIRST EDITION

Following the establishment of the European Economic Community, a Committee of Experts was set up under the Chairmanship of Pierre Uri to prepare studies of the economic conditions of the member countries. The report on the economic situation in the countries of the Community was published in 1958. Following the accession in 1973 of Denmark, Ireland and the United Kingdom, the Commission of the European Communities considered that it would be valuable to supplement the Uri Report with a study on each of the new member States. On this occasion, however, the Commission followed a somewhat different procedure and commissioned separate studies from independent institutes in each of the three countries.

The present study of the United Kingdom was prepared at the National Institute of Economic and Social Research, London. The authors of the various chapters are named on the title page, but, in addition, mention should be made of the contributions of Miss G. I. Little, who prepared the text for publication and compiled the bibliography, and Miss S. Colwell, who typed the draft chapters as well as the final text. Thanks are due to Miss Patricia Brown of HM Treasury and her colleagues in government, as well as to H. R. Wortmann of the Commission of the European Communities, for valuable comments, and criticism, of draft chapters. The responsibility for the final version remains with the authors.

G. D. N. Worswick
National Institute of Economic and Social Research
January 1975

PREFACE TO THIS EDITION

In this new edition the text and the figures have been brought up to date, which in most cases means the end of 1977. In some chapters parts of the text have been substantially rewritten and there are consequential changes in the list of authors.

We are grateful to the Commission of the European Communities for allowing us to make the study available in the present form.

G. D. N. Worswick
National Institute of Economic and Social Research
December 1978

Chapter 1

GENERAL FEATURES

1. Introduction

In the nineteenth century the British economy was expanding in production, trade and overseas investment both in absolute terms and in its relative importance in the world. During the twentieth century, notwithstanding the setbacks of two world wars and the great depression, the upward trend in production and trade has been maintained, but outward investment has been increasingly offset by inward flows. In relation to the rest of the world, however, the story of production and trade has been one of fairly steady relative decline. Partly this is a simple matter of demography, which can most vividly be seen by comparing the populations of the United Kingdom and the United States over the whole period as in Table 1.1. Population movements alone made relative economic decline inevitable; but, in addition, the growth-rate of output per head in Britain has tended frequently to be somewhat lower than the average for other industrial countries of Western Europe and for the United States. This poor *relative* performance has been very much emphasized in the past twenty years, during which statistics of national product on a reasonably comparable basis have become increasingly available.

Britain was a pioneer, and for a long time the leader, in the process of industrialization which began at the end of the eighteenth century. Already by the middle of the nineteenth century its urban population was as large as that remaining in the countryside, and from then on food and raw material needs for a growing population in industry were increasingly supplied from overseas in exchange for manufactured goods. By the end of the nineteenth century British exports provided one-third of the world's trade in manufactures. Throughout the nineteenth century there was also a net export of capital: at times a trickle,

Table 1.1. *Populations of the United Kingdom and the United States compared, 1801-1977*

				Millions
	1801	*1851*	*1901*	*1977*
United Kingdom	11.9	22.3	38.2	55.9
United States	5.5	24.1	77.6	216.5

at others a torrent. To begin with it went mostly to Europe and the United States, then to Canada and India, and at the end of the century to Australia and Latin America. In the earlier stages money was invested mainly in public works, utilities and, above all, railways; later it was extended to industry and manufacturing enterprises. Besides money there was an increasing outflow of iron and steel, engineers, contractors and technology. In the decades before the First World War British overseas investment was of the same order, in *absolute amount* as American private investment abroad in the 1960s. But already, at the height of its economic dominance, comments were being made which have become a commonplace today, that British industry was technically backward and was being overtaken by other countries, notably the United States and Germany.

The two world wars, the slump in the 1930s and the oil crisis in the 1970s administered great shocks to the world economy and to the British economy in particular, so that twentieth-century economic development cannot be easily summarized in a few simple trends. While the period between the two wars was one of small growth and high unemployment, for twenty-five years after the Second World War there was full employment and gradually accelerating growth. A single instance must suffice to illustrate this uneven development. In 1901 British steel output was just short of 5 million tons and in 1913 it had risen further to 7.7 million tons. Output fell immediately after the war, but this level was again surpassed in the late 1920s. However, in the early 1930s steel output was once again down to 5 million tons, no higher than it had been thirty years before. By contrast, after the Second World War the expansion of steel production, as indeed of many other industries, was strong; with output at 13 million tons just before the Second World War, it was over 20 million tons by the end of the 1950s.

Exports of manufactures reached a peak volume in 1913. The war sharply curtailed them and, even in the boom year of 1929, they had still not recovered their prewar level. The great depression dealt a further blow, as it did to world trade in general, so that British export levels in the early 1930s were little more than half those of 1913. But after the Second World War the recovery of exports was strong and continued; 1913 levels were surpassed in the early 1950s and they have gone on rising almost continuously. This uneven development in the twentieth century was, of course, matched in many other industrial countries. The *share* in world trade of British exports of manufactures started to fall at the beginning of this century; it jumped up again temporarily immediately after the Second World War while Germany and Japan were largely out of the picture. Thus, in 1950 the British share in exports of the main industrial countries was still 25.5 per cent, little short of the 27.3 per cent taken by the United States. But as Germany and Japan began their spectacular recoveries, the United Kingdom share started to fall once more, so that by 1960 it was down to 16 per cent and in 1973 for the first time it fell below 10 per cent.

The massive overseas investment at the beginning of this century dried up between the two wars, although it was to revive again after the Second World War until the most recent period. Meanwhile, dividends and interest from past investments played a significant role in the 1920s and 1930s in paying for necessary imports at a time when exports were performing none too well. During the Second World War large amounts of the investments were disposed of to pay for arms and when the war was over it was apparent that from then on current earnings from British exports, visible and invisible, would need to be at least sufficient to pay for current imports. The balance of payments has been a matter of concern for the economy since 1945 much more than in the previous century.

Judged by its own historical standards the economic performance of the United Kingdom in the past quarter of a century has been good. Unemployment was kept very low and the productivity of those employed rose annually at around 2 per cent in the early 1950s and at around 3 per cent in the early 1970s. This performance, however, appears in a different light when set against that of other industrial countries, most of which have had higher growth-rates, and some very much higher.

Following renewed hostilities between Egypt and Israel in 1973, the Arab oil producing countries for a while curtailed supplies to the industrial world. OPEC, the organization of oil exporting countries, within a very short period raised the price of crude oil between four and five times and, while the restriction on supplies was shortlived, the price rise persisted. Coming towards the end of a boom in the industrial countries, which had already set off a sharp rise in commodity prices, the oil crisis precipitated the longest and deepest recession since the Second World War. The loss of output and the scale of unemployment were not as dramatic as in the slump of the 1930s; on the other hand, the rate of inflation, which had jumped sharply in the preceding boom, remained obstinately high. In consequence, the recovery throughout the world was slower in coming and proved altogether more hesitant than on previous occasions since 1945.

The British economy experienced a severe set-back to begin with from the oil crisis. The terms of trade, which had already deteriorated as the result of rising commodity prices, were further worsened by the oil price increase. Whereas before a quantum of imports required three units of exports, by 1974 this had become four units. Production stagnated, unemployment rose to nearly 1½ million; and inflation worsened

even more than elsewhere. By 1978, however, recovery was clearly dis-
cernible, aided by a new factor, namely the discovery of North Sea oil.
Intensive exploration and development in the early 1970s led to an
increase in production in the second half of the decade, and it was
expected that by 1980 the United Kingdom would have become
self-sufficient in oil. One aspect of this development was the partial
recovery of the terms of trade. Nevertheless, both unemployment and
inflation remained higher than in the 1950s and 1960s and it was an
open question whether the path of full employment accompanied by
slowly accelerating growth would be resumed, or whether Britain, and
possibly the industrial world as a whole, had entered a new phase of
slower growth and persistent unemployment.

The dominant economic philosophies in nineteenth-century Britain
were *laissez-faire* and free trade. The major exception was in the monetary field, in which the Bank of England, though nominally remaining a
private institution, emerged in a strong position of central control.
Although mergers and industrial concentration were causing some concern at the end of the nineteenth century, there was no legislation
laying down rules of competition of any general application until the
1950s. In the 1930s, however, there were several instances of specific
government intervention to alleviate the problems of particular industries, especially the staple industries of the previous great industrial
expansion, such as coal, cotton and shipbuilding, which were in decline.
This growth of government intervention was closely associated with the
abandonment of free trade in the 1930s. Since the Second World War
there has been a considerable further increase in the role of the State in
industry; important sectors such as transport, public utilities, coal and
steel have been nationalized, and various forms of intervention and
assistance for the private sector have been developed, especially in the
context of regional policy; at the same time there has emerged a more
systematic policy towards monopolies and restrictive trading agreements.

From the end of the Napoleonic Wars until the outbreak of the First
World War the pound sterling was convertible into gold at a fixed rate
which remained unchanged. After wartime suspension, convertibility
was restored at the old rate in 1925, but this restoration was shortlived,
the final break between sterling and gold being made in 1931. The gold
standard, combined with complete freedom of movement of goods,
services and people into and out of the country, had encouraged the
growth in London of specialist banking, insurance and shipping firms
able to arrange for the financing and movement of goods in almost any
part of the world. In addition there developed important markets in
many commodities. The business of the City of London has been, and
still remains, an important influence towards internationalism in British
economic policy.

The interests of industry and agriculture have not always pointed in the same direction. To begin with the advantage of cheap food, especially from the newly developing agricultural regions of North and South American and Australasia, outweighed any arguments in favour of protection. But the two world wars put a premium on protection of agriculture and the experience of mass unemployment in the 1920s, and especially the 1930s, reinforced other arguments in favour of protection for industry, which was finally introduced soon after the abandonment of the gold standard.

One consequence of the British decision to leave the gold standard was to require those countries which had previously held their reserves in sterling (and thus indirectly in gold) to decide whether they wished to continue to hold reserves in sterling or to remain on the gold standard at the old rate. In the case of British colonies it was possible for this decision to be taken in London. The independent dominions, with the exception of Canada, decided to stay with sterling and so did the Scandinavian countries. This sterling bloc was the forerunner of the Sterling Area, which was formalized under the exchange control systems introduced during the Second World War. Partially overlapping with this Sterling Area was the Imperial Preference Area (subsequently the Commonwealth Preference Area), created at negotiations in Ottawa in 1932, the effect of which was to increase the share of both British exports to and British imports from Commonwealth countries.

Several, not always consistent, lines of thought lie behind British international economic policy in the past thirty years. The first was a desire to restore the importance of Britain in world trade and the world's monetary system. This led to support of the Bretton Woods monetary agreement and of the parallel Havana Charter of International Trade, which ultimately emerged in the more modest General Agreement on Tariffs and Trade (GATT). A premature attempt was made to restore full convertibility of sterling in 1947, but failed within a matter of weeks. Thereafter even the most ardent British advocates of the principles of Bretton Woods and GATT accepted that it might take some years before the various wartime controls of imports and monetary transactions could safely be removed altogether. It was not in fact until 1958 that Britain was observing the full principles of the International Monetary Fund (IMF) and GATT.

A second strand of opinion was towards the maintenance, and if possible the strengthening, of the Commonwealth connection. Although many colonies were achieving political independence, it was thought that their economic development would be assisted by maintaining a close association with one another and with the United Kingdom. This Commonwealth approach was in some degree in conflict with the GATT philosophy which, while tolerant of customs unions, was hostile to preference areas.

The third line of thinking was the desire to secure closer economic relations with Europe, especially Western Europe. The idea of a free trade area for manufactures caught on quite early, particularly as it was felt to be consistent with other objectives, such as those of GATT. There was less universal support for other aspects of the European Economic Community (EEC) such as the Common Agricultural Policy (CAP), partly because it was thought to conflict with the historic policy of cheap food and the Commonwealth commitment.

In the early 1970s the Bretton Woods international monetary system of predominantly fixed exchange rates was already crumbling; in 1972 it was abandoned altogether, to be replaced by floating exchange rates, managed in different degrees by different countries. Accompanying this change was the final disappearance of the old Sterling Area. Britain's external policy choices narrowed and became increasingly concerned with whether or not to join in particular developments originating in the EEC.

British domestic policy since the war has been to secure the establishment of a welfare state. The first requirement of this was the maintenance of full employment, an objective which seemed never to be seriously threatened until the 1970s, but which has been put in question by the oil crisis and the sharp increase in the rate of inflation which has occurred throughout the industrial world. There has been a great extension of social services, in health and education especially, while industrial policy has been based upon the concept of a 'mixed economy' of private and public enterprises. For a long time after the war the two major political parties, both of which formed several governments, appeared in practice tacitly to accept a common central programme with differences of emphasis. In the past five years, however, the power in the two main parties may have been shifting away from the centre in opposite directions. The years ahead will show whether some radical transformation in British industry and society is about to occur or whether some new consensus will emerge.

2. Demographic Trends

The population

In comparison with the very rapid expansion of population which took place in the nineteenth century, there has been a relatively slow increase throughout this century. From 1801 until 1911 the population increased in each decade by at least 10 per cent, but since 1911 the increase in each decade has never been more than about 5 per cent. The natural increase in population was at its highest in absolute terms from 1901 to 1911, when births exceeded deaths by 4.7 million. In the inter-

Table 1.2. *The United Kingdom population, 1901-2011*

	Home population (000s)	Increase		Net immigration[a] (000s)
		Absolute (000s)	Percentage (%)	
1901	38,237 ⎫			
		3,845	10.1	−820
1911	42,082 ⎭			
		1,945	4.6	−919
1921	44,027 ⎫			
		2,011	4.6	−672
1931	46,038 ⎭			
		4,187	9.1	+445
1941	n.a.			
		2,484	4.9	+ 57
1951	50,225 ⎫			
		2,806	5.3	−428
1961	52,709 ⎭			
1971	55,515	87[c]	0.2	−320
1981	55,697[b]			
		1,015	1.8	−400
1991	56,712[b]			
		923	1.5	−400
2001	57,535[b]			
		171	0.3	−400
2011	57,706[b]			

SOURCE: CSO, *Annual Abstract of Statistics, 1977*.

[a] Including various adjustments for the visitor balance and armed forces living abroad.

[b] Projections of mid-year 'total population'.

[c] Not equal to the difference between the figures in the first column because of changes in definition.

war years the net increase fell to 2.0 million (1921-31) and then 1.8 million (1931-41). Since the war the net decadal increases have been 2.5 million (1951-61) and 2.8 million (1961-71). The increase in population over those last ten years was 5.3 per cent, which is slightly higher than the increase of 4.9 per cent in the 1950s (see Table 1.2), but official projections of the population over the next four decades from 1971 expect a slower rate of increase of 0.2 per cent (1971-81), 1.8 per cent (1981-91), 1.5 per cent (1991-2001) and 0.3 per cent (2001-11).[1] These projections mean that the population of the United Kingdom, estimated to be 56.0 million in mid-1975, would fall to 55.7 million by 1981, but rise to

[1] Central Statistical Office, *Annual Abstract of Statistics, 1977*, London HMSO 1977, table 21.

57.7 million by 2011. However, such projections are constantly changed. The birthrate in recent years has been falling much more sharply than expected by those who prepared the offical projections, so that with each successive fall the projections of future population have been brought down. The laws concerning abortion have recently been changed, and the principle of the free provision of contraceptives has been spreading. It is therefore highly uncertain what the average completed family size will be for couples now in their twenties and thirties. In 1975 the official projection for the increase in population in the last quarter of the century was 3¾ million. By 1977 it had already been revised downwards to less than 2 million and may be changed again.

Migration, both inward and outward, has been an important influence on United Kingdom population. For the first thirty years of this century there was an average net emigration of almost 100,000 a year; in the next ten years (1931-41) there was a net inflow of 600,000. During the 1950s there was an almost equal balance between emigration and immigration — a net inward balance of 57,000 over the ten years 1951-61. A large number of the immigrants came from the West Indies, East and West Africa, and India and Pakistan, but there were always large numbers of Irish immigrants as well. Since the Commonwealth Immigrants Act of 1962 and further restrictive measures which followed it, immigration has been severely restricted and outward migration has considerably exceeded immigration. Over the decade 1961-71 there was a net emigration of 428,000, but this figure masks the yearly movements; in 1961-2 there was a net inflow of 300,000, whilst since 1962 there has been a large net outflow of, on average, some 60,000 persons a year. The official population projections assume a future net outflow averaging about 32,000 a year in 1971-81 and a further 40,000 a year to the end of the century.

The female population continues to be larger than the male, despite the greater number of male births (outweighing female births in the ratio of 1.06 to 1), because of the higher male mortality, but the gap between males and females is narrowing. The 1951 population was 48.0 per cent male, so that there were 4 per cent more females than males, by 1971 this gap had narrowed to 2.8 per cent, with 48.6 per cent males; the projections for 2001 indicate a male population of 49.3 per cent and hence a gap of only 1.4 per cent. For all age groups under 45 the male population now outnumbers the female population, although in no case by more than about 6 per cent. In the older age groups the position is reversed and females outnumber males by successively greater amounts.

The age composition of the United Kingdom population has changed quite radically through this century. Partly because of successively longer life expectancies, the proportion of people aged 65 and over has been rising. In 1911 5.2 per cent of the population were aged 65 and over, by 1971 this figure was 12.9 per cent. It is expected to continue to rise but

Table 1.3. *The age composition of the United Kingdom population, 1911-2001*

| | Absolute size | | | Proportion of total | | |
| | Under 15 | 15-64 | 65+ | Under 15 | 15-64 | 65+ |
		(millions)			(percentages)	
1911	13.0	26.9	2.2	30.9	63.9	5.2
1931	11.1	31.4	3.4	24.2	68.4	7.4
1951	11.3	33.4	5.5	22.5	66.5	11.0
1961	12.3	34.1	6.1	23.4	64.9	11.7
1971	13.6	35.4	7.3	24.2	62.9	12.9
1981a	*11.3*	*36.1*	*8.3*	*20.3*	*64.8*	*14.9*
1991a	*11.4*	*36.8*	*8.5*	*20.2*	*64.8*	*15.0*
2001a	*12.5*	*36.8*	*8.2*	*21.8*	*64.0*	*14.2*

SOURCES: CSO, *Annual Abstract of Statistics, 1977*, Table 2.3; Office of Population Censuses and Surveys, *Population Projections 1976-2016*, London, HMSO, 1978.
aProjections of total population at mid-year.

then fall back to around 14 per cent by the end of the century (see Table 1.3). The corollary to this is that the proportion of people under 65 years of age has fallen and, because the trend since the war has been for the proportion of the population aged under 15 to increase slowly (22.5 per cent in 1951, but 24.2 per cent in 1971), this has meant that the proportion of the population aged 15-64 has fallen substantially, from 66.5 per cent in 1951 to 62.9 per cent in 1971. In other words, since the war the population has tended to become both top- and bottom-heavy. This is regarded as unfavourable in so far as it means that the part of the population which is of working age has shrunk, but this unfavourable trend is not expected to persist. It had two causes: first, the low interwar birth rate, which has meant a relative decline in the number of middle-aged persons, and, secondly, the slightly higher birth rate of the late 1950s and the 1960s. The first will eventually result in a fall in the proportion of the old, whilst the second has been reversed in just the last few years. The second also means that there are more people of working age in the 1970s. These factors taken together mean that the forty-year decline in the proportion of 15-64 year olds in the population will be reversed in the mid-1970s. Official projections suggest that this proportion will rise from its 1971 level of 62.9 per cent (a historic low) to 64.8 per cent in 1981 and then fall back to 64.0 per cent by 2001. One cannot put much confidence in these projections, but one can at least say that the unfavourable movement in the age structure should now come to an end.

Employment

The changing demographic structure of the population, as indicated, has meant that since the 1930s a decreasing proportion of the population has been of working age. This is one of the reasons why the working population has not kept pace with the growth in the total population. Until just recently the working population has not only declined as a proportion of total population but has also declined in absolute terms (see Table 1.4). Several further reasons have been put forward to explain why this has happened. The main arguments concern, first, the marked trend in the number of young people who are continuing their education beyond the minimum school-leaving age and, secondly, variations in participation rates.

The proportion of the population in the age group 15-19 attending grant-aided schools in Great Britain has risen from 9 per cent in 1951 to just over 25 per cent in 1972. Furthermore, since 1972 the minimum school-leaving age has been raised from 15 to 16, which means that an estimated further 0.4 per cent of the total population has been removed from the working population. Besides this increase in the amount of schooling undertaken beyond the age of 14, there has been a rapid expansion of full-time further education. In particular, there has been a boom in university education, especially in the years since 1961. The number of full-time students at United Kingdom universities rose from 87,000 in 1951-2 to 117,000 in 1961-2, and then more than doubled in the next ten years to 243,000 in 1971-2. A similar expansion took

Table 1.4. *Working population and activity rates in the United Kingdom, 1901-71*

	Working population thousands	Activity rates							
		Males and females					*Females*		
		15-19	*20-24*	*25-44*	*45-64*	*65+*	*20-24*	*25-44*	*45-64*
						(percentages)			
1901	18,280	n.a.[a]	76.0	61.1	55.5	34.1	56.7	27.2	21.1
1931	20,930	77.6	80.7	62.5	54.7	25.3	65.1	30.9	19.6
1951	23,809	81.3	79.7	66.7	59.5	15.9	65.4	36.1	28.7
1961	25,345	72.9	76.8	69.4	66.0	12.7	62.0	40.8	37.1
1966	26,174	68.6	77.2	72.6	60.6	13.1	61.6	47.1	46.1
1971	25,421	58.4	75.1	74.4	71.5	11.3	60.1	50.6	50.2

SOURCES: Department of Employment, *British Labour Statistics: historical abstract 1886-1968*, London, HMSO, 1971; *Department of Employment Gazette*, November 1973.

[a]Statistics not available because of uncertainty over ages at which juveniles started work.

place in other establishments of further education. The result has been that a very considerable number of young persons who would previously have been entering the work-force are now continuing with their education. This trend is reflected in the activity rates for the 15-19 age group: in 1951 81.3 per cent of this group were economically active: this fell to 72.9 per cent in 1961 and to 58.4 per cent in 1971.

An examination of activity rates for different age groups (as in Table 1.4) shows that, although since the war the proportion of persons economically active has declined for those aged under 25 and for those over 64, nevertheless the 25-64 age group has increased its rate of activity quite substantially. In particular there has been a large and continuing increase in the proportion of women aged 25-64 in the work-force. This has mainly been due to the much higher number of married women who now work; since 1931 their activity rate has increased from 10 per cent to nearly 50 per cent. This increase in the female participation rate meant that the percentage of women in the total working population increased from 32.0 per cent in 1951 to 36.0 per cent in 1971. Yet, despite this large increase in female participation, the working population has still been a declining proportion of the total population, because the lower participation of the younger and older age groups has proved a stronger force. Indeed these latter effects have been so strong that the total working population declined in absolute terms between 1966 and 1971. However, as the age structure of the population has 'improved' through the 1970s, this trend has been reversed.

Unemployment, which was rarely less than 10 per cent throughout the interwar years, has normally been below 3 per cent and rose above 4 per cent for the first time since the war only in mid-1975. Nevertheless, there has been a slow secular movement towards higher levels of unemployment throughout the postwar period; the peak level has slowly risen through successive cycles. In the early 1950s the peak rate was 2.2 per cent (1952); but in the 1967-73 cycle this had risen to 3.9 per cent (1972), and in the present cycle has risen to 6 per cent (1977). Similarly at troughs, the unemployment rate has tended to move upwards through successive cycles. Various reasons have been put forward to explain this phenomenon: it is thought that higher unemployment compensation and compulsory redundancy payments have meant that the unemployed worker is not faced with the same urgency to find a job as in the past; it is also thought that firms may now carry fewer under-employed staff, especially in slack periods. There has also been a noticeable rise in graduate unemployment, particularly amongst social scientists, but it is not certain how far this reflects an over-supply of new graduates, or how far it is the outcome of an unwillingness to take up employment immediately after graduation.

A feature of the unemployment pattern is the great disparity between the various regions. Northern Ireland, for instance, has consistently had a much higher rate of unemployment than the rest of the United Kingdom. In 1972, whilst the average rate of unemployment for the United Kingdom was 3.9 per cent, that for Northern Ireland was 8.0 per cent. Two other regions, Scotland and the North of England, have also tended to have rates of unemployment well above the average — in 1972 rates of 6.4 and 6.3 per cent respectively. This is in sharp contrast to the South East where, until 1975, unemployment has never been more than 2.1 per cent (1972) in the postwar period and has at times been less than 1.0 per cent, for example in 1964-6. East Anglia, the Midlands and the South West have also been areas where unemployment has been much less than the national average. These regional disparities have been partly the result of the decline of the older consumer goods industries, such as textiles and clothing, and of mining, shipbuilding and other heavy industries, all of which have been concentrated in the regions such as Scotland, the North, the North West and Wales which now exhibit above-average unemployment levels. In these less prosperous regions there is a lower activity rate and a much smaller proportion of female manual workers than in the rest of the country. Although there is only a rather slow movement of the population within the United Kingdom, it is noticeable that the movement is towards areas of high incomes and job vacancies (the South East and the Midlands) and away from areas of low incomes and higher unemployment (especially Northern Ireland, Scotland and Wales).

3. National Product and its Uses

United Kingdom output

Since the war the average growth-rate of GDP for the United Kingdom has been about 2½ per cent per annum. This is higher than at any other comparable period this century, but is nevertheless lower than that of any other major industrialized country. There has been a marked cyclical pattern in the rate of growth, but only four years of actual decline (1952, 1958, 1974 and 1975). There have been six cycles over the last twenty years: 1951-5, 1955-60, 1960-5, 1965-9, 1969-73 and the present cycle from 1973[1] Nevertheless the trend rate of growth has remained fairly constant.

Growth-rates in individual sectors have differed widely from the overall average (Table 1.5). Until the mid-1970s there had been an absolute decline in the mining and quarrying sector, which was at a

---

[1] Peak to peak. The dating of these cycles is taken from D. J. O'Dea, *Cyclical Indicators for the Postwar British Economy*, Cambridge University Press, 1975, and from CSO, *Economic Trends*.

postwar peak in 1954. This trend has recently been reversed with the introduction since 1975 of North Sea oil, which is recorded in the industrial production statistics in the mining and quarrying sector. There are also plans, in the light of the oil price rise and the energy situation generally, to increase coal output in the next few years from the present 120 million tons annually to 150 million tons.

Construction has been an industry which has grown very slowly since the war, and it has actually shown a marginal decline over the period 1967-77. Public administration and defence has also grown slowly, although the size of the public sector as a whole has grown substantially. Other sectors which have grown at less than the national average are agriculture and the distributive trades.

Output of the manufacturing sector has grown at a rate of 2.4 per cent per annum over the period 1957-77. Within the sector particular industries have grown at very disparate rates and these are examined in the following section. The largest growth-rates, however, have been recorded in non-manufacturing; gas, electricity and water have grown

Table 1.5. *United Kingdom GDP by industry*

| | GDP 1977 | | Annual growth-rates | |
	Value (£m)	Proportion of total (%)	1957-77 (%)	1967-77 (%)
Agriculture, forestry and fishing	3,447	2.7	2.2	1.6
Mining and quarrying	3,627	2.9	0.8	3.7
Manufacturing	35,279	27.8	2.4	1.5
Construction	8,062	6.3	1.2	−1.4
Gas, electricity and water	4,296	3.4	4.6	3.9
Transport	6,641	5.2 }	2.7	2.6
Communication	3,603	2.8 }		
Distributive trades	12,657	10.0	2.0	1.3
Insurance, banking and finance	9,171	7.2	4.6	3.8
Ownership of dwellings	7,787	6.1	2.3	2.5
Public administration and defence	9,159	7.2	0.7	1.2
Professional and scientific services				
Miscellaneous services	23,332	18.4	2.7	2.4
Total	127,061	100.0		
Residual error	−4,791			
Adjustment for financial services	1,083			
GDP at factor cost	123,353		2.4	1.9

SOURCE CSO, *National Income and Expenditure*, London HMSO, (annual).

by 4.6 per cent per annum, the same as insurance, banking and finance. The latter sector now constitutes 7.2 per cent of total output (1977 figures) compared with 27.8 per cent for manufacturing and 40.4 per cent for total industrial production. Agriculture, forestry and fishing now provide only 2.7 per cent of output, and mining and quarrying 2.9 per cent; public administration, defence, health and education provide 14 per cent and transport, communication and the distributive trades 18 per cent of output − roughly the same share as in 1950. The ownership of dwellings, at 6.1 per cent, is now a more important component of output than it used to be, whilst construction, at 6.3 per cent, has about the same importance.

Productivity changes in these various sectors have meant that the pattern of employment has not necessarily mirrored the changes in output. Although agriculture has continued to grow, its total labour force (employers and employees) has more than halved from about 1.5 million in 1950 to under 700,000 in 1978. In the same period employment in all service industries (SIC Orders XXII-XXVII) has risen from 8.9 to 12.6 million. Whilst agriculture has undoubtedly seen a very rapid rise in productivity, in services productivity has increased only slowly. There has also been a decline between 1950 and 1978 in the numbers employed in manufacturing, and that sector now accounts for 32.5 per cent of the total numbers in civil employment, whereas previously it accounted for 41.0 per cent. Since output in manufacturing was growing faster than average over the period, this reflects a substantial increase in productivity in the sector. Another particularly productive sector has been gas, electricity and water, where the numbers employed have fallen only slightly and output has grown rapidly. In mining and quarrying there has been a large fall in employment, from 855,000 in 1950 to 340,000 in 1978; this reflects not only the large fall in output before North Sea oil production, but also a marked rise in productivity. Despite the large increase in government work, the number of employees in the public sector (public corporations, central and local government) has risen little, from 6.2 million in 1950 to 7.4 million in 1977, although in the earlier year there was still a large residue of the wartime civil service.

Output broken down by final demand
Rather less than half of total final expenditure (45.4 per cent in 1977) is accounted for by consumption, but the proportion has been slowly declining since the 1950s (Table 1.6). Exports have been an increasingly important component of final expenditure, rising from 15.4 per cent to 22.7 per cent between 1957 and 1977. The other major component of demand, public authorities' current expenditure, has shown a large fall in its relative share, from 19.4 per cent in 1957 to 16.8 per cent in

Table 1.6. *United Kingdom expenditure and output at 1975 market prices, 1957-77*

| | Contribution to final demand | | | | | Value |
| | 1957 | 1962 | 1967 | 1972 | 1977 | 1977 |
			(percentages)			(£m)
Consumer's expenditure	51.7	52.3	50.0	49.5	45.4	62,732
Public authorities current expenditure	19.4	18.1	17.5	16.1	16.8	23,315
Gross domestic fixed capital formation	12.9	14.6	16.9	16.0	14.3	19,738
Stockbuilding	0.6	—	0.5	—	0.8	1,051
Exports of goods and services	15.4	15.0	15.1	18.4	22.7	31,357
Total final expenditure	100.0	100.0	100.0	100.0	100.0	138,193
Less *imports of goods and services*						30,276
GDP at market prices						107,917

SOURCE: CSO, *National Income and Expenditure.*

1977; this is largely explained by the falling proportion of output taken by military defence. However, this masks the position of the public sector as a whole, which has grown in importance since the 1950s. When transfer payments like debt interest, pensions, social security payments and grants to industry are included, the public sector now controls, directly and indirectly, the way in which half of the national product is spent. The rise in public spending on this wider definition has been especially rapid since the 1960s; in 1965 public spending as a share of GNP (at current prices) was 39.0 per cent, by 1975 this had risen to 52.8 per cent, but it then fell back to 47.7 per cent by 1977. The change in the importance of the public sector is examined in greater detail in Chapter 4.

The trend in consumers' expenditure since the early 1960s has been for a relative decline in spending on the necessities — food, clothing, housing, fuel and light — and for greater spending on consumer durables. At 1975 prices, household expenditure on food declined quite sharply from 21.7 per cent of consumption in 1967 to 19.2 per cent in 1977; spending on drink and tobacco has marginally increased its relative share in consumption over the same period (rising from 10.9 per cent to 11.9 per cent), but this disguises the rapid growth in consumption of wines and spirits, and the actual decline in sales of tobacco throughout most of the period. Similarly, the increase in expenditure on durables, from 6.8 to 7.4 per cent, masks a static share of furniture sales and a large rise in spending on radio and electrical goods and, until the oil crisis, on cars and motor cycles.

4. Regional Differences

The regions into which the United Kingdom is divided for statistical purposes are Northern Ireland, Scotland, Wales and eight standard regions of England. They are so delimited that most of them contain a major urban core and in no region is the population predominantly rural. Although it is still possible to find quite extensive rural areas where agriculture is the largest single occupation, the regions with the largest reliance upon agriculture are Northern Ireland and East Anglia, neither with more than 10 per cent of their active population in this pursuit. The dichotomy, so important in many countries, between predominantly agricultural and non-agricultural major regions does not exist in the United Kingdom.

The historical origin of the differences in structure and prosperity between the regions is to be found in developments during and since the Industrial Revolution. Urbanization, which has been proceeding at varying rates for at least four centuries, has brought a continuous increase in the proportion of the total population in and around London, which now dominates an extensive city region — the South East — containing almost a third of that total. From the mid-eighteenth century, however, until the beginning of the twentieth, a proportionately more rapid growth took place in industrial areas outside the South East, based in many instances upon coalfields. The most spectacular development was in the North West, based largely upon the cotton textile industry, followed by Yorkshire and Humberside (wool textiles, steel and coal) and the West Midlands (metal working). The North (coal, steel and shipbuilding) and Wales (coal and steel) followed long-term trends in growth not very different from that of the country as a whole. Scotland and Northern Ireland, despite very substantial industrialization, declined in population in relation to the United Kingdom total — Northern Ireland for a long time declined absolutely. Throughout this period up to the First World War, the industrial regions of Wales, the Midlands and the North of England drew in a net immigration of population, or suffered less from emigration overseas than did the less industrialized regions of the South West and East Anglia; they also seem to have had higher wage levels and (in the early twentieth century) lower unemployment. Scotland and Northern Ireland, with, at that time, still large populations in low-income agriculture, continued long-established traditions of heavy outward migration, largely overseas.

The industrial areas outside the South East had owed their growth in the main to foreign trade and shipbuilding. However, the heavy British commitment to foreign trade, prolonged in the face of rising foreign competition by massive overseas lending, was sharply checked by the First World War and its aftermath. The effects of this check were concentrated on those regions in which the exporting industries were localized. On any reasonable interpretation, the relative depression of these industrialized areas in the last fifty years has been due primarily to their inherited industrial structure. It is not only that they originally relied upon industries that have suffered in world markets; the rapid growth in the last two generations has, to a large extent, been in non-manufacturing activities, of which a substantial part (central government, professional and scientific services, head office activities, the handling of air traffic, entertainment, specialized aspects of banking and finance) has a strong tendency to establish itself near the national capital. Another rapid grower, the motor vehicle industry, found in the West Midlands and the South East the varied metal-working activities best suited to providing its components, and thus increased still more the relative disadvantage of the regions further north. Moreover, once differences of prosperity are established various forces operate to accentuate them. Some of these are greatly reduced in the United Kingdom by the extent to which a progressive tax system and central provision of social services and infrastructure prevent poorer regions from falling too far behind in the facilities they offer, but old industrial regions with low growth-rates almost inevitably present a less attractive appearance to new industry than fast-growing ones, or those regions like the South West and East Anglia with in most parts little industrial dereliction.

Table 1.7 *Rates of employment growth by region, 1921-61 and 1965-76*

Percentages

	1921-61	1965-76
North	10.8	−1.2
Yorks. and Humberside	7.9	−5.0
North West	1.3	−7.3
East Midlands	26.5	3.0
West Midlands	39.9	−6.3
East Anglia	20.4	13.3
South East	41.3	−2.9
South West	29.3	4.0
Wales	0.3	−3.2
Scotland	1.0	−2.1
Northern Ireland	−4.6[a]	6.9

SOURCE: NIESR estimates based on Censuses of Population and Department of Employment.
[a]For the period 1926-61.

From the end of the First War to the early 1960s employment in the four regions south of the Trent and east of the Severn grew relatively quickly, that in the North and in Yorkshire and Humberside much more slowly and that in the remaining regions hardly at all (in Northern Ireland there was a fall). In the later period 1965-76, when national employment underwent a (partly cyclical) decline of about 2½ per cent, the pattern was different. The South East and the West Midlands ceased to grow (the latter, indeed, declined considerably); the main growth area moved to the neighbouring regions of East Anglia, the South West and the East Midlands. The North West showed a considerable decline and the remaining regions declined slightly, with the exception of Northern Ireland which grew markedly (see Table 1.7).

Differences in income *per capita* between regions are smaller in the United Kingdom than in most other countries; only Northern Ireland shows a really large departure from the national average. In factor income *per capita* Northern Ireland stands some 36 per cent below the average, but all the other regions lie within about 12 per cent above or below it, and the interregional flow of property incomes, which is in favour of the richest region (the South East) as well as of one of the otherwise poorer ones (the South West), makes the range of gross regional product *per capita* somewhat greater than that of domestic factor incomes.

The distribution of expenditure is, however, markedly affected by taxation and those parts of public spending that can be identified as being mainly beneficial to particular regions. As in other fairly centralised modern economies, public finance reduces interregional differences in *per capita* incomes by about 40 per cent. Private capital transfers on balance work in the same direction. Distribution is further modified in real terms by the fact that the general price level is appreciably higher in London and the South East than elsewhere, mostly because of the higher costs of accommodation and travel to work. When all this is taken into account, it seems that real expenditure per head is considerably less than 20 per cent below the national average in Northern Ireland and elsewhere lies within 7 or 10 per cent of it.

This relatively high degree of interregional uniformity of income and expenditure levels is due in the first place to the absence of a division of regions into urban and rural which has already been mentioned. Agriculture, as happens in other countries also, is the least well paid occupation, but not by as large a margin as in most European countries; moreover, it does not bulk large enough in any United Kingdom region either to pull the average down very far arithmetically, or to depress earnings in other industries very much through market forces. The compactness of the United Kingdom and the national scope of much collective bargaining in its labour market tend to standardize wages in an industry across the different regions. In general, the industrial mix rarely accounts for much of the excess or deficiency of a region's earnings level in comparison with the national average.

In unemployment levels the interregional differences are much more important; indeed, it may be argued that the tendency to interregional standardization of the price of labour makes deficiency of regional demand manifest itself in unemployment rather than low wages. Ever since the First World War unemployment has been lowest in the South East (and usually the Midlands) and highest in Scotland, Wales, Northern Ireland and the North of England. Between the two world wars, when unemployment was generally high, it stood about twice as high in the latter group of regions as in the former. From 1945 to 1965, when absolute levels were very low, the relative (but not absolute) differences were somewhat greater than this; in the period of higher unemployment since 1966 the reverse has been the case. The situation in 1977, a year of high unemployment, was as shown in Table 1.8.

Table 1.8. *Rates of unemployment, 1977*

	Percentages
North	8.4
Yorkshire and Humberside	5.8
North West	7.5
East Midlands	5.1
West Midlands	5.8
East Anglia	5.4
South East	4.5
South West	6.9
Wales	8.1
Scotland	8.3
Northern Ireland	11.2

SOURCE: *Department of Employment Gazette.*

A broad correlation between rapid growth and low unemployment has persisted, though it is far from perfect; the South West, for instance, has not shown one of the lowest rates even when growing fastest — partly because seasonal unemployment there tends to be high. The greater imperfection of the labour market in less densely populated regions may also be of some importance, but differences in pressure of demand, rather than in labour-market imperfection, or in the incidence of inherent unemployability in the labour force, seem to be the main factor determining regional unemployment differences.

The recorded rates of registered unemployment do not tell the whole story. According to Census data, there is a body of unregistered unemployed so distributed between regions as to raise considerably the absolute, but not the relative, interregional differences in the incidence of involuntary worklessness. More important quantitatively, however, is the wide interregional variation in participation rates of women in the labour force — varying from under 30 to nearly 45 per cent, though this difference has tended to diminish.

The largest population movements have been relatively short-distance ones out of the conurbations and large cities, but these have mostly intra-regional rather than interregional significance. Interregionally, the *net* internal movements, which consist of differences between gross inward and outward movements several times as large, have followed a fairly simple pattern. In the 1960s every region gained from those to the north of it and lost to those to the south, except for large net movements from the South East to the neighbouring regions, East Anglia, the East Midlands and the South West. The last mentioned region is the only one that has tended to show a net gain from every other one; Scotland is the only one except for Northern Ireland that has lost to every other. The effects of these internal movements have been reinforced in general by the fact that nearly every region of England and Wales has gained from overseas migration (with the South East and the West Midlands gaining most), while Scotland has lost heavily. Taking internal and overseas movements together, Scotland in the 1960s lost more than 6 per thousand of her population a year (almost equal to her natural increase), Northern Ireland lost more than 5 per thousand (50 per cent of natural increase) and the North 3 per thousand (60 per cent of natural increase). The South West and East Anglia were gaining from migration at about the same proportional rate as that at which Scotland was losing; the South East and the West Midlands had become slight net losers.

In general, gross interregional migration movements (leaving overseas movements out of account) seem to be reasonably well 'explained' statistically by the sizes of existing populations in the regions of origin and destination, the existence or non-existence of proximity between them, and their unemployment rates. The relation of migration movements to average income levels in the regions is less close; most notably the regions with the highest gains from migration (the South West and East Anglia) are relatively low-income regions. The earnings of migrants in their regions of origin and destination do not seem to be representative of the general levels in those regions.

The distribution of industry in the last two or three decades has followed trends very different from those of the nineteenth century. There has been a strong tendency for industries to grow faster or decline more slowly in the regions where they are less strongly represented — in other words, diversification of regional industrial structure and dispersion of individual industries has been the tendency, rather than specialization and localization. To some extent this simply reflects the relative decline of industries that had previously become highly localized, but that accounts for only part of the trend; regional policy, too, may account for some of it. In general it seems likely, however, that the tendency is mainly due to the increasing extent to which modern manufacturing industry is 'footloose', because of the improvement of transport and communications, the changing nature of industry and the compact geography of the country. The tendency to cluster together in a central situation has been stronger recently in some service activities than in manufacturing industry proper; hence much of the continued growth of the South East. Latterly, however, market forces, together with some encouragement from policy and perhaps from faster transport and better communications, have produced a considerable dispersion of office work. This has, as yet, however, mostly been confined to within a hundred miles of London.

Regional policy, to which some passing references have already been made, is of long standing in the United Kingdom. The first manifestation of it — rather different in form from later ones — was the measure introduced in 1928 to assist movement of labour from areas of heavy unemployment to job-opportunities elsewhere. It was abandoned after a decade. Meanwhile, from 1934 other measures began to be taken to encourage movement of job-opportunities to the most depressed areas and, modest though these measures were, there were signs that they were producing some results immediately before the Second World War.

The war itself largely suspended regional differences in prosperity by producing general full employment, moving activity towards peripheral areas and stimulating some of the localized industries, for example shipbuilding, which had been in decline. However, thinking about postwar policy proceeded on the assumption that the prewar problems would return. The Barlow Report recommended government control of the location of new industrial establishments,[1] and the White Paper on employment policy gave some support to such measures.[2] Subsequently, the Town and Country Planning Act of 1947 gave the Board of Trade power to control new industrial building through the issue of Industrial Development Certificates, and the Distribution of Industry Act, operative from the previous year, gave powers for various forms of assistance — grants, loans, renting of government factories — to developments expected to create employment in the designated Development Areas.

With the assistance of some remaining wartime powers and in the presence of postwar shortages of buildings and manpower, regional policy made a powerful impact on the distribution of industry in the

---

[1] Royal Commission on the Distribution of the Industrial Population, *Report*, Cmd 6153, London, HMSO, 1940.

[2] *Employment Policy* Cmd 6527, London, HMSO, 1944.

first five postwar years; but thereafter, with the slackening of controls and shortages, and in the absence of the expected early return of depression in the old exporting industries, its effect weakened. The recession of 1958 marked the re-emergence of the regional problem as an evident matter for concern and policy measures began to be strengthened. The greatest single strengthening came in 1963, when measures were introduced that amounted to differential assistance of something over 15 per cent to typical capital expenditure on industrial establishments in the assisted areas. The form of assistance was changed, but its cost not greatly altered, by the Act of 1966, which also redefined the Development Areas as large, coherent entities containing collectively about a fifth of the manufacturing industry of Great Britain. (The government of Northern Ireland applied parallel but somewhat stronger incentives.) In 1967 there was added the Regional Employment Premium, a subsidy amounting initially to about 7.5 per cent on manufacturing wages in the Development Areas. Two years later, following the report of the Committee on Intermediate Areas,[1] a new class of area was introduced in which benefits were available on a reduced scale. A class of Special Development Areas had already been introduced in 1967, mainly comprising districts in which coalmining employment was declining especially fast, to which certain additional assistance was given. (As a different type of measure, office development in the more prosperous areas had been controlled since 1964.)

In 1970 the form of assistance was changed and its amount greatly reduced. The emergence of heavy and substantially localized unemployment in the following year, however, prompted the introduction in 1972 of benefits not very different in scale from those of the late 1960s. The new measures, besides benefits which were automatic, provided also for selective assistance to industry, including in some cases mobile service establishments. Later measures of regional significance have mostly taken the form of assistance to particular firms with establishments in the assisted areas. The armoury of inducements to industry to move into or expand in the assisted areas is thus now quite a formidable one. On the other hand, it must be noted that in recent years the stringency of control over industrial building by Industrial Development Certificates has been considerably relaxed, most notably by the raising of the minimum size of development for which a certificate is required and the abandonment of this control in Development Areas.

In addition to the financial incentives and the restrictions that have been briefly described, there have been attempts at the promotion of development by the direct provision of facilities. The building of

---

[1] Department of Economic Affairs, *The Intermediate Areas*, Cmnd 3998, London, HMSO, 1969.

government factories to rent to industrialists in some degree at concessionary terms was one of the earliest and has been one of the continuing strands of regional policy — fairly modest in scale, but broadly successful. The building of new towns, originally conceived as a means of relieving pressure of population in the overcrowded conurbations, developed, especially in Scotland and the North, and later in central Lancashire, into an attempt to provide 'growth-points' for the economic rejuvenation of respective regions. Additional central government assistance in the removal of industrial dereliction and the modification of the pattern of road development in the interests of areas in need of an economic stimulus have also played some part in general regional policy.

Specific measures of this kind can certainly be effective in particular cases, especially where the whole pattern of settlement in an area needs to be changed to make it suitable for modern industrial activities. But, in a closely settled industrial country with a very extensive (even though often old) urban infrastructure, the problem of renewing growth is very different from that in, for instance, a country that is bringing large rural populations into non-agricultural work. One lesson of experience in the United Kingdom seems to be that rather strong incentives, perhaps supplemented by prohibitions, are needed to direct development into regions that are physically not badly equipped to support it, but would not attract it through the working of market forces alone. Governmental opinion seems, implicitly, to have swung back to this view, after an interval in which the desirability of operating mainly through the provision of infrastructure and the establishment of growth-points was favourably considered.

In view of the determination with which some kind of regional policy has been pursued over a long period, it is important to know, if possible, how effective it has been. It is not, of course, practicable to say with confidence what would have happened in any period without any regional policy at all, the more so since there has been no period for a long time in which the effects of regional policy can be presumed to have been negligible. The latest period of strong policy, since 1972, has not yet lasted long enough for its effect to be assessed and the prolonged period of low activity since 1974 makes assessment difficult. But studies have been made of the change — assumed to be largely due to policy — between the 1950s, when policy was relatively weak, and the middle and late 1960s, when it was stronger. In this interval big changes came about both in the pattern of 'moves' (including the establishment of branches) by manufacturing industry and in the regional distribution of industrial building. Changes can also be detected in the regional distribution of employment growth when that part of it attributable to differences in regional industrial structure is eliminated.

The upshot of such studies is that, between the two decades in question, growth of employment in the assisted regions was augmented by various amounts between 15,000 and 40,000 a year in manufacturing industry, which might have been expected to bring substantial secondary increases in employment growth also. It seems reasonable to suppose that the policy operated from the middle 1960s is responsible for a good deal of the changed pattern of total employment growth which Table 1.7 showed and the convergence of unemployment rates referred to above.

What seems to emerge, then, from a consideration of the regional problems of the United Kingdom is that the relative mildness of interregional differences and migration flows has owed much not only to the compensating effects of centralized public finance and the compactness of the country, but also to specifically regional policy. Without that the story would have been very different.

It may be added that from the mid-1970s public and governmental anxiety about location of economic activity has shifted largely to concern at the plight of inner city areas, from which movement of population and, still more, of employment opportunities has been particularly rapid. In the South East and the West Midlands the broad brush of regional policy has no doubt exacerbated this problem; in the assisted regions it has not been sufficiently strong or precise to deal with it. The new layer of policy which has begun to be introduced to deal with the inner cities, however, must be regarded as largely independent of regional policy as described above, which is concerned with the treatment of differences between the major areas of the country.

Chapter 2

THE MAIN SECTORS

1. The Industrial Sector

Industrial production
Industrial production has accounted for about 40 per cent of GDP in the recent past. Before the fall in output in 1974 and 1975, the normal pattern was that industrial production would grow slightly faster than GDP, whilst manufacturing production would, in turn, grow rather faster than total industrial production. The main reason for industrial production lagging behind manufacturing was the steady decline in mining and quarrying experienced until 1974. However, since then the output of mining and quarrying has more than doubled under the impact of North Sea oil. This, combined with the continuing strong growth in gas, electricity and water, has led to a reversal of the old pattern with industrial production growing faster than manufacturing since 1975.

Within the manufacturing sector, two industries have suffered an absolute decline since the war, shipbuilding and marine engineering, and leather and fur. Output of these industries is now about 25 per cent and 16 per cent respectively below the level of output in 1956. Metal manufacturing output is lower now than 20 years ago as a result of only slow and erratic growth in 1957-73 and of a sharp fall since then caused by the worldwide metal recession. Other slow-growing industries have been other metal goods and textiles. It is these industries — shipbuilding, mining, textiles and metals — which were the basis of Britain's early industrialization; now they are of fading importance.

The food, drink and tobacco industry grew at 2.2 per cent per annum from 1957-77, but with the drink and tobacco sector expanding much faster than food. Paper, printing and publishing grew at a slightly slower rate than manufacturing, recording a 2.1 per cent growth-rate between 1957 and 1977 — rather less than the 2.7 per cent for bricks, pottery, glass and cement. The other medium-growth industry has been vehicles, which grew at 3.0 per cent per annum up to 1973, although, because it was so badly hit in the period 1974-6, its growth over the period 1957-77 is barely over 1 per cent per annum.

The engineering industries have experienced a rapid growth in the postwar period. Technical developments have meant that the leading industries have been instrument and electrical engineering, with growth

Table 2.1 *United Kingdom industrial production (output)*

	1975 weights	Annual growth-rates	
		1957-77	1967-77
		(percentages)	
Food, drink and tobacco	77	2.2	1.8
Coal and petroleum products	9	3.4	2.1
Chemicals and allied industries	57	5.7	4.8
Metal manufacture	47	−0.2	−1.2
Mechanical engineering	92	2.3	1.0
Instrument engineering	12	6.2	4.7
Electrical engineering	66	4.6	3.5
Shipbuilding and marine engineering	14	−1.2	−0.7
Vehicles	68	1.1	0.2
Other metal goods	46	1.0	0.8
Textiles	40	0.7	0.9
Leather and fur	3	−0.9	−0.6
Clothing and footwear	24	1.3	1.7
Bricks, pottery, glass and cement	28	2.7	1.3
Timber and furniture	25	2.4	1.0
Paper, printing and publishing	58	2.1	1.1
Other manufacturing	31	5.0	3.7
Total manufacturing	697	2.3	1.6
Construction	182	1.3	−1.3
Gas, electricity and water	80	4.6	4.0
Mining and quarrying	41	0.7	3.5
Total industrial production	1000	2.2	1.5

SOURCE: CSO, *National Income and Expenditure 1967-77*, London, HMSO, 1978.

rates of 6.2 and 4.6 per cent per annum respectively over the period 1957-77, compared to 3.3 per cent per annum for engineering as a whole. The development of new weapons systems, the spread of new domestic appliances, the electrification of the railways, the development of new scientific instruments and increasing computerization have meant a substantial and continuing demand for the output of these industries and in particular its electronics section. Mechanical engineering, though still the most important of the engineering sector, producing about 55 per cent of engineering output, has been growing much more slowly (2.3 per cent per annum between 1957 and 1977).

Technical developments have also been the major factor responsible for chemicals and allied industries being a fast growing sector. Plastics and similar materials have replaced metals in many uses and synthetic materials have replaced natural fibres in the textile industry and else-

where; new products have been introduced and other products modified using chemical-based compounds. The result has been that these
industries have grown at 5.7 per cent per annum in the last twenty years.

The output of coal and petroleum products has also grown quite
rapidly due to the growing demand for oil products in all walks of life.
Of course the substitution of new chemical-based products for old has
meant that metal manufacture, leather and fur, cotton textiles and
similar industries have suffered accordingly; hence their below-average
rates of growth. Metal manufacture has also been hit by the decline of
its traditional user industries, such as shipbuilding, the railways, defence
and heavy engineering generally.

A further industry, not so far mentioned, is other manufacturing,
which has been growing at a rate of around 5 per cent per annum. This
above-average growth can largely be explained by increased demand for
rubber (for cars, flooring, etc.) and for plastic products not elsewhere
specified, which together account for most of the output of the sector.
The sector also includes toys and sports equipment, and these too, at a
time of rising incomes and increasing leisure, have been growing extremely fast.

The figures for capital expenditure and employment (Table 2.2)
show that, whilst industrial and manufacturing output has been growing
at around 2½ per cent per annum in the last twenty years, the inputs of
labour and capital have grown at widely different rates. The employment figures for the period 1959-77 show that the number of workers
in manufacturing has fallen by about 0.5 per cent per annum. This is in
sharp contrast to the growth in capital, which, over the same period,
has been about 3 per cent per annum. (The figures for total industry
follow the same pattern.) Within manufacturing, however, there have
been large differences in the growth of employment and capital in
different sectors.

The largest increases in the capital stock in the last twenty years
have occurred outside manufacturing in construction and mining and
quarrying, the latter increasing very fast in the 1970s with the development of North Sea oil. Within manufacturing, the fastest increase in
capital in the period 1959-77 has been in bricks, pottery, glass and
cement, where the capital stock has grown by 5.5 per cent per annum
on average. Much of this investment has been in the glass industry,
where the float glass process has been a major innovation.

Heavy capital investment has also taken place in the chemical
industry, one of the fastest growing sectors. Here the growth in capital
has been at an average annual rate of 4.3 per cent (this figure includes
capital growth in coal and petroleum products which are slower growing), which corresponds closely to the growth in output over the same
period. In recent years fixed capital expenditure in the chemical industry

Table 2.2 *United Kingdom industrial production (inputs)*

	Employment[a]			Capital[b]	
	1978 (000s)	*Annual growth-rates (%)*		*Annual growth-rates (%)*	
		1959-77	*1967-77*	*1959-77*	*1967-77*
Food, drink and tobacco	719	−0.3	−0.5	4.2	3.9
Coal and petroleum products	37	−2.3	−1.0	4.3	3.9
Chemicals and allied industries	431	—	−0.3		
Metal manufacture	459	−1.1	−2.2	3.4[c]	3.0[c]
Mechanical engineering	935	−0.1	−1.3		
Instrument engineering	149	0.5	−0.8		
Electrical engineering	749	0.6	−0.9		
Shipbuilding and marine engineering	184	−2.3	−0.5	2.7[c]	2.2[c]
Vehicles	775	−0.6	−0.6		
Other metal goods	540	0.3	−0.8		
Textiles	498	−2.6	−2.3		
Leather and fur	40	−1.9	−2.2	1.8[d]	2.4[d]
Clothing and footwear	382	−1.7	−1.6		
Bricks, pottery, glass and cement	268	−0.9	−1.7	5.5	3.8
Timber and furniture	264	−0.3	−0.3	4.3	4.4
Paper, printing and publishing	543	−0.1	−1.1	3.0	2.8
Other manufacturing	336	1.4	1.0	...[d]	...[d]
Total manufacturing	7309	−0.5	−1.0	3.2	2.9
Construction	1258	−0.5	−1.8	6.4	4.8
Gas, electricity and water	350	−0.5	−1.9	3.5	2.2
Mining and quarrying	344	−4.7	−4.3	6.4	9.6
Total industrial production	9261	−0.7	−1.3	3.4	3.1

SOURCES: Department of Employment, *British Labour Statistics Yearbook 1975*, London, HMSO, 1977; CSO, *Monthly Digest of Statistics* and *National Income and Expenditure 1967-77*.

[a]All employment figures relate to June each year.
[b]Gross capital stock at 1975 replacement cost.
[c]Iron and steel only in metal manufacture; other metals included with engineering and allied industries.
[d]Includes also other manufacturing.

has been about the same as that of the whole of engineering and ship-building, whose output is three times that of the chemical industry. This partly reflects the technical complexities of many modern chemical processes, but is also one of the reasons why the industry has expanded so rapidly.

There has been, perhaps surprisingly considering its relatively low growth rate, substantial capital expenditure in the food, drink and tobacco industry, where the capital stock has grown on average by 4.2 per cent per annum. The development of new products, the growth of the market for frozen food and packeted convenience foods, and the rapid growth of the drink and tobacco sector have been responsible for this heavy investment.

The only industries where there has not been a decline in employ-ment in the period 1959-77 are instrument and electrical engineering, other metal goods and other manufacturing. Chemicals employment is at the same level as in 1959. With the exception of other metal goods, these are the sectors with the fastest growing ouptut. Among the in-dustries showing a fall in employment, only shipbuilding, coal and petroleum products, mining and quarrying, textiles and clothing and footwear have steadily reduced their work-forces. For the remaining industries, the pattern showed gradual growth in employment until the late 1960s or early 1970s, with a rapid decline in labour in the recent years. This fall in manufacturing and industrial employment (of −1.6 and −1.9 respectively between 1966 and 1977) corresponds with a 0.3 per cent per annum growth in the working population.

So far as actual numbers employed are concerned, the engineering industries still dominate manufacturing employment, with over 2 million workers (1978) out of a total of just over 7.3 million in manu-facturing as a whole. There are also 775,000 in the vehicles sector and 1 million in metals and other metal goods. Despite the declining work-force, textiles and clothing are still very labour-intensive and together employ some 900,000 workers. The other large employing sectors are food, drink and tobacco with 719,000 workers and paper, printing and publishing, where there are 543,000 workers. Outside manufactur-ing, there are 1.3 million working in the construction sector, although the work-force has been contracting slowly, and there are still 344,000 in the mining and quarrying sector despite its rapid decline. The rede-ployment of miners has been a problem, because as recently as 1959 there were some 750,000 employees in the mining and quarrying sec-tor, but ironically in the last few years the problem in the coalmines has been the failure to retain labour rather than redundancy.

There has been a relative decline in the importance of industrial employment in the total, while experience has varied considerably between different regions (see Chapter 1).

Concentration

This section gives a brief review of the recent trends in industrial concentration, both in the aggregate and in individual markets, together with a short survey of government policy towards monopoly and restrictive practices. Most studies of concentration have been concerned with possible monopoly power in the hands of private companies; consequently the nationalized enterprises, including public utilities, coal-mining and, since 1968, the iron and steel industry, have been excluded. (In 1968 employment in the iron and steel industry accounted for roughly 4 per cent of the total in manufacturing industry.)

The changes in aggregate concentration, that is in the manufacturing and distribution sector as a whole, enable us to gauge the changing importance of the largest privately owned enterprises in the economy. Two estimates suggest that in the first half of this century the level of aggregate concentration increased moderately, and in fact probably fell during the decade spanning the Second World War. Measuring aggregate concentration by the relative dispersion of publicly quoted companies in manufacturing, mining and distribution, Hart and Prais found a significant increase between 1896 and 1939, but by 1950 relative dispersion was little different from that at the turn of the century.[1] Similarly, in a study of the hundred largest firms in manufacturing industry, Prais estimated that their share in the total net output of the sector rose from 16 per cent in 1909 to only 24 per cent in 1935. By 1949 the share had fallen slightly to 22 per cent.[2] It is possible that wartime planning controls ensured a larger share of output for smaller firms than would otherwise have occurred and that this helped to interrupt, in the period 1939-50, the long-term moderate rise in concentration.

Since 1950 the upward trend has not only been resumed but has shifted very markedly. By 1973 the hundred largest enterprises accounted for 42 per cent of the net output of the manufacturing sector.[3] As a group they have therefore nearly doubled their share in a little over twenty years. There is no simple explanation of why the rate of aggregate concentration should have accelerated so sharply, but a number of statistical analyses have established that, compared with the remarkable rise in the share of the largest *enterprises* in manufacturing net output, the share of the hundred largest *plants* (or establishments) has remained

---

[1] P.E. Hart and S.J. Prais, 'The analysis of business concentration: a statistical approach', *Journal of the Royal Statistical Society* (series A), vol. 119, part 2, 1956.

[2] S.J. Prais, *The Evolution of Giant Firms in Britain*, Cambridge University Press, 1976.

[3] The figures from 1970 onwards are based on a somewhat wider coverage than for the earlier years, but this does not alter the main conclusion in the text.

more or less unchanged at 10-12 per cent for the last forty years (the longest period for which estimates can be made). The demands of technology forcing firms to build mammoth plants in order to take advantage of production economies of scale cannot, therefore, be held responsible for the increase in the concentration of the enterprises. (This is not to say, of course, that the absolute size of the largest plants has not increased.)

On the other hand, since the late 1950s and early 1960s, several studies have indicated that larger firms have been growing on average proportionately faster than smaller firms. In the first half of the century there was no such systematic tendency. An important factor that probably helps to explain this faster proportionate growth, and hence the concentration increase, is merger activity among large firms. Since the early 1960s mergers have increased substantially in volume and importance, reaching a peak in 1968 and again in 1972.

A number of studies have shown that upwards of one half of this increase in aggregate concentration was probably due to mergers, although with the onset of recession in 1974 the level of merger activity declined considerably. Measured in real terms, the consideration paid for acquisitions of industrial and commercial companies in the period 1975-77 was only about one third of that during 1970-72.[1]

Taken together these points suggest that the accelerating increase in concentration in manufacturing has been caused by the larger firms maintaining a faster proportionate growth than smaller firms, a process assisted by widespread acquisition and resulting in a substantial rise in the number of plants operated by the largest firms.

Market concentration does not *have* to rise simply because aggregate concentration has increased. For example, the largest firms in manufacturing could increase their share of the sector's output as a whole by diversifying their activities across a wide range of markets without causing significant individual increases. In view, however, of the extent of the recent increase in aggregate concentration, such a result would be surprising, especially as it is known that the largest firms in absolute size are frequently amongst the leaders in individual markets. The measurement of market concentration can be an important first step in assessing the extent of monopoly power in individual industries, but two preliminary points should be noted. First, the level of seller concentration in a market is only one of several important characteristics of market structure which have a bearing on monopoly power. Of equal importance are, for example, the conditions of entry, the extent of product differentiation and the level of buyer concentration. Secondly,

---

[1] Department of Prices and Consumer Protection, *A Review of Monopolies and Mergers Policy*, Cmnd 7198, London, HMSO, 1978.

data from the Census of Production, which are frequently used to measure market concentration, suffer from a number of well documented shortcomings for the purpose in hand and these should be borne in mind when considering the results discussed below.

Detailed studies of market concentration using the material from the Census of Production have been made covering the period 1935-75. Comparisons over time of concentration levels for individual products or product groups (which we refer to as 'market concentration') meet a formidable number of problems, but the result is reasonably well established that market concentration rose fairly persistently throughout the period, although the latest available data suggest that the rate of increase may have slowed in the 1970s. Thus the average concentration ratio (the share of total sales made by the five largest firms) for comparable sets of products or product groups increased between 1935 and 1951, between 1951 and 1958 (for a different set of products) and again between 1958 and 1975. By 1975 the five-firm average concentration ratio had reached just over 65 per cent, only marginally above the comparable figure for 1968.

These figures refer to the average change throughout product groups in manufacturing industry. But perhaps of more significance for the problem of monopoly power is the growing importance of very highly concentrated products — those where the five largest firms account for 80 per cent or more of total United Kingdom output. In 1958, in a sample of 214 product groups in manufacturing, about 18 per cent of sales was accounted for by groups where the five-firm concentration ratio was 80 per cent or more; the comparable figure for 1963 was 24 per cent of sales. An important increase also took place between 1963 and 1968. In a comparable sample of 288 product groups, those heavily concentrated accounted for just over 34 per cent of total sales in 1963, but for 39 per cent by 1968. The latest available figures relate to 1975 and in that year, out of a sample of 271 product groups for which full information is available, there were 98 with a concentration ratio of 80 per cent or more and these accounted for 41 per cent of the sales of the total sample.

On the face of it these figures hint at a widespread potential for the exercise of monopoly power, either through the market share of a single dominant seller or through tacit oligopolistic price co-ordination. While the concentration figures alone are sufficient to raise important policy questions, it must be stressed that they provide only a first step in the full analysis of market structure, which ideally requires a detailed case-study approach. Apart from the qualifications already made above, it is also important to note that Census of Production data refer only to United Kingdom output and hence do not take account of imports, which are clearly an important source of competition in many cases.

Between 1960 and 1977, for example, imports of manufactured goods as a percentage of home sales increased nearly threefold from 5.4 per cent to 15.9 per cent (measured in constant prices). Also the recent *Review of Monopolies and Mergers Policy* lists thirty manufacturing industries where the concentration ratio was reduced by 10 percentage points or more when adjusted to the account of foreign trade.[1] While domestic *output* may thus be heavily concentrated, a sizeable proportion of *sales* in the United Kingdom may be made by foreign competitors. What appears initially as an industry open to monopolistic abuse may on closer inspection be highly competitive.

The approach of British competition policy since the war has been, broadly speaking, to view each case on its merits. The policy entered a new phase in 1973 with the passing of the Fair Trading Act, which created a Director General of Fair Trading, with overall responsibility for co-ordinating policy on competition and consumer affairs through the new Office of Fair Trading. To appreciate more fully the scope of that office we sketch below the main elements of British policy since 1948.

Until the creation of the Monopolies Commission in 1948,[2] there was no modern law which sought to regulate or control possible abuses of market power. In that year the Monopolies Commission was empowered, at the direction of the Board of Trade, to investigate how 'the public interest' was affected in industries where one firm or a group of firms acting together controlled one-third or more of the United Kingdom market. There was no presumption in its inquiries against large market shares or in favour of competition and the definition of what constituted 'the public interest' was left deliberately vague and largely up to the Commission to decide. Its reports presented a detailed historical and contemporary analysis of the industries investigated, with, if necessary, recommendations to Parliament as to how the public interest could be better served in the future. Most of its earlier reports were concerned with cartels rather than individual positions of dominance. It was the knowledge gained in these inquiries of the particularly damaging effects on actual or potential competition that could follow the close regulation by restrictive agreements among producers

---

[1] Ibid, Table 9. In these adjustments it was assumed that the five leading firms in each industry (a) made no imports of finished products of the industry, and (b) were responsible for the same proportion of exports as of domestic output.

[2] Over the years the title of the Commission has changed. Originally it was the Monopolies and Restrictive Practices Commission; in 1956 it became the Monopolies Commission and in 1973 the Monopolies and Mergers Commission. For convenience we refer to it throughout as the Monopolies Commission.

of prices, outputs, discounts, authorized dealers and other matters that led to the next stage of British policy. The Monopolies Commission had performed the valuable service of making public the extent and probable effects of a wide range of restrictive practices; the subsequent task was to ensure that any abuses were corrected.

The 1956 Restrictive Trade Practices Act provided for the registration of all restrictive agreements and their scrutiny by the specially constituted Restrictive Practices Court. The register, which is open to public inspection, was maintained by the new Registrar of Restrictive Agreements. In two important aspects this section of the 1956 Act marked a new departure: first, the fact that a Court could hear cases of this kind was a 'revolutionary step in British constitutional law and procedure'; secondly, the restrictive agreements were deemed to be against the public interest unless the Court was convinced otherwise on one or more of a number of grounds laid down in the Act. The grounds are that: (a) it protects the public from injury; (b) the public derives a benefit from it; (c) it offsets the restrictive practice of another firm or trade association; (d) it enables producers to negotiate fair terms with a monopoly buyer; (e) employment *or* (f) exports would suffer if it were abandoned; (g) it maintains another restriction upheld by the Court. If the Court accepts the argument for the maintenance of the restriction on one or more of these grounds, it then has to be satisfied that the restriction is not unreasonable having regard to the balance between these circumstances and any detriment to the public or to persons not parties to the agreement. Thus, there is a general presumption in favour of competition except where this is rebutted. In 1964 the practice of resale price maintenance was brought within a similar procedure under the Resale Prices Act.

On the face of it the success of the 1956 Act appears to have been remarkable. By the middle of 1972, for example, a total of 2,620 registrable agreements had been ended, or modified so as not to infringe the Act. Similarly resale price maintenance had been almost universally abandoned. But, as overt (and registrable) agreements were ended, there was growing concern about the use of 'information' agreements, which did not formally come within the machinery of the 1956 Act, but which might enable firms to achieve the same degree of collusion. Consequently an attempt was made in 1968, in a further Restrictive Practices Act, to bring such agreements within the scope of the Court by providing for the registration and possible scrutiny of certain classes of such agreements. In the view of the authors of a recent study of the effects of the restrictive practices legislation, as far as information agreements were concerned 'the 1968 Act seems to have delivered the final *coup de grace*; by this time it seemed evident that generally industry had decided to drop what remained [of their restrictions] rather than register'.[1]

For a period in the late 1950s and early 1960s the control of restrictive practices rather overshadowed the residual tasks of the Monopolies Commission in examining positions of market dominance. However the increase in merger activity in the 1960s, noted above, rapidly produced a major policy response. In 1965, the Monopolies and Mergers Act empowered the Board of Trade (now the Department of Prices and Consumer Protection) to refer to the Monopolies Commission for investigation mergers which involved the creation or increase of a market share in the United Kingdom of at least a third, or where the assets acquired were valued at £5 million or more. There were special provisions for mergers involving newspapers. At the end of its inquiries (which normally can last up to six months) the Commission has to recommend whether or not the merger is likely to operate against the public interest. If the conclusion is that the merger is likely so to operate, the Department has the power to prevent the merger, to unscramble it if it has already taken place, or to allow it to proceed subject to conditions.

The whole basis of British policy was placed on a firmer foundation by the 1973 Fair Trading Act, which superseded the previous legislation in this field and brought the several strands of policy together under the authority of the Director General of Fair Trading. His department has become the focal point for the collection of information and the initiation of action. Thus he now has power to make references on monopolies to the Monopolies Commission. The scope for inquiry by the Monopolies Commission has also been widened in several ways under the 1973 Act: for example, firms having 25 per cent (rather than one-third as previously) of the United Kingdom (or local) market can now be referred, also nationalized enterprises; restrictive agreements relating to *services* have to be registered and may be the subject of a case in the Restrictive Practices Court. The Director General of Fair Trading is chairman of the committee that decides which mergers to recommend for reference to the Monopolies Commission and he assumes full responsibility for proceedings under the Restrictive Practices Acts. Thus, as one authority put it soon after the passing of the Act, 'for the first time, the implementation of the monopolies and restrictive practices legislation will be brought together, so that the Director General should be able to take a more comprehensive view of the working of competition in the economy than either the Department of Trade and Industry or the Registrar have been able to do in the past'.[2]

---

[1] D. Swann, D.P. O'Brien, W.P. Maunder and W.S. Howe, *Competition in British Industry*, London, Allen and Unwin, 1974, p. 163.

[2] E.L. Smith, 'The Fair Trading Act', *Trade and Industry*, 9 August 1973, p. 304.

The growing evidence on the extent of the increases in aggregate and market concentration and concern over Britain's international competitiveness prompted a wide-ranging review of monopolies and mergers policy at the end of 1977. The results, published in the middle of the following year, put special emphasis on mergers.[1] As we have seen, mergers are thought to have played a central role in the concentration increase and had been brought within the scope of policy in 1965. In fact, the great majority of mergers that came within the 1965 Act were judged *not* to raise issues warranting reference to the Monopolies Commission and were allowed to proceed without full investigation. Excluding newspaper mergers (which have special provisions), 43 mergers were referred to the Commission between 1965 and the first quarter of 1978 out of more than 1500 that came within the scope of the legislation. Of these, only fourteen were found to be against the public interest, fifteen were abandoned and fourteen were considered to be *not* against the public interest. 'Thus under 2 per cent of the mergers falling within the legislation have been prevented by present policy although the very existence of the legislation may have deterred others from taking place.'[2]

The main recommendation of the *Review* was that in future, policy should take a neutral view of mergers rather than the generally favourable one that had prevailed hitherto. In addition to increasing the number of mergers investigated by the Commission (initially as much as fourfold), the proposals were intended to ensure that important mergers were better thought out, so that a convincing case could be made to the Department, or to the Commission in the event of a reference. Other areas suggested for further study (oligopoly, uncompetitive practices, labour practices and international competition) are likely to produce further proposals for policy reforms. The importance that the government attaches to an effective competition policy is thus clearly demonstrated.

2. The Services Sector

Britain, like the United States before it and others besides, is nowadays becoming a service economy. The distinction between 'goods' and 'services' is not sharply defined. Should transportation be regarded as an integral part of goods production or as a service? The repair of a pair of shoes undertaken on the premises of a retail establishment would count as a service, but if the shoes were sent back to the manufacturer the repair would probably count as goods. Nevertheless, a rough division of industries is illuminating. Leaving aside agriculture,

---

[1] Department of Prices, *A Review of Monopolies and Mergers Policy*, para. 3.31.

[2] Ibid, para. 3.31

which in Britain is in any case small, we classify as 'goods industries', mining, manufacturing and construction, and then treat all the rest as services. On this basis 13.2 million people were employed in services and 8.9 million in goods in the United Kingdom in 1976. If we were to transfer transport and communications to the goods side, however, the service sector would be only slightly larger than the goods sector. Moreover, the figures here refer to employees in paid employment and exclude self-employed persons. The use of Census of Population data would raise a little the share of services in total manpower, but a slightly different picture again would be given if output were used rather than employment or manpower as the measure.

As a rule there is wider fluctuation in goods employment than in services, a difference especially marked in the interwar period. This fact, combined with the shadowy nature of the line separating goods from services,[1] makes it difficult to discern trends, but it appears that in the United Kingdom there was a tendency for service employment to grow faster than goods employment in the interwar years, a tendency reversed by the war, when the distributive trades especially lost a substantial part of their manpower to the armed forces and war production. Since the war, and especially since the 1950s, the comparatively faster growth of service employment has been renewed. In the most recent period in fact service employment has continued to rise, while goods employment has actually been falling. In Table 2.3 we show the industries here classed as services, with the employment in them for two recent years, 1969 and 1976, and the change between those years. At the foot of the table we give the total of goods employment, that is in mining and quarrying, manufacturing and construction, in the same two years.

The recent rise in employment in insurance and banking and in catering and hotels draws attention to another way of looking at the importance of services in the economy. In 1977 visible exports were valued at £32.2 billion; in the same year credits for sea and air transport, travel and other private services were £11 billion; that is Britain earned abroad a third as much by selling services as by selling goods. On the other hand, the expenditure on private services of £7.4 billion was just over a fifth of the outlay on visible imports of £33.9 billion. There is in fact normally a substantial surplus on invisible account (which includes other items as well as services) to offset the deficit on visible account. The earnings of financial institutions, commonly called 'the City', are of particular interest. Total credits in 1977 were £1.4 billion, the biggest items being insurance and banking; similar earnings in the United

---

[1] In the reclassification of manpower which took place in 1959, 700,000 men who had been listed under manufacturing under the old Standard Industrial Classification of 1948 were transferred to distribution.

Table 2.3. *United Kingdom employment in service industries compared with total in goods industries, 1969 and 1976*

| | Employees | | Change |
| | 1969 | 1976 | 1969-76 |
	(thousands)		(%)
Gas, electricity and water	406	353	−13.1
Transport and communications	1,561	1,475	−5.5
Distributive trades	2,711	2,723	+0.4
Insurance, banking and finance	893	1,103	+23.5
Professional and scientific services	2,849	3,654	+28.2
Catering and hotels	710	850	+19.7
Miscellaneous services	1,284	1,449	+12.8
Government service			
National	598	660	+10.4
Local	867	966	+11.4
Total in service industries	11,879	13,233	+11.1
Total in goods industries[a]	10,249	8,902	−13.1

SOURCE: CSO, *Monthly Digest of Statistics*, August 1978, Table 3.2.
[a]Mining and quarrying, manufacturing and construction.

Kingdom by overseas financial institutions were negligible. We should note that North Sea oil is rapidly replacing imports of oil, so that in future there will be a near balance in goods and a large surplus in services; there will however also be a larger negative item to cover payments of profits to overseas oil companies.

The reasons for the comparative growth of service employment in advanced countries are well known. As a rule, rising real income leads to a disproportionate rise in the demand for services. Moreover, over long periods the manpower requirements for given outputs tend to fall more slowly in services than in manufacturing. There are plenty of exceptions to this, and there is also a tendency for services previously marketed to be replaced by self-service, as a result of which part of service output may be taken out of the national accounts. On balance, service employment is likely to rise in relation to goods employment even faster than the relative rise in output. Income elasticities are obviously a strong factor in explaining the growth of service employment, but there have been complementary explanations, for example, that the structure of markets is more conducive to restrictive practices in service trades, which are thus less competitive and less prone to introduce labour-saving advances, although, of course, it is not easy to see how the labour 'productivity' of such services as hairdressing or gravedigging can easily be improved.

The measurement of output and productivity in service industries is notoriously difficult. John Gorman has shown, for instance, that if the business of banks is regarded as the production of money for people to hold, then, in the United States over the period 1948 to 1966, measured productivity was *declining* at annual average rate of 1.5 per cent; whereas if one takes the view that the banks' primary business is the facilitation of spending, then measured productivity has been *increasing* at an annual average rate of 2.75 per cent.[1]

Different methods of calculating productivity change yield varying results, but they all tend to show a slower trend in the increase of labour productivity in most service trades than in goods. A similar difference has been noted in the United States, Canada and elsewhere.

A. D. Smith gives estimates of annual average changes in labour productivity over the period 1951-66 (Table 2.4). British indirect taxation has traditionally fallen on commodities, especially because purchase tax, introduced during the Second World War and continued since, fell mainly upon manufactured goods. Until 1966 very little indirect taxation fell upon services. This bias against manufactures was partially redressed by the introduction in 1966 of the selective employment tax, a tax on employment in certain service trades. This imposed on employers in some industries a tax of a certain amount per week for each person they employed, varying according to whether the worker was adult or juvenile, male or female. The administration was somewhat complicated in as much as the amount of the tax was added to the weekly National Insurance contribution paid by all employers for all employees irrespective of their trade, but then employers in defined industries were allowed a refund (initially with a premium in the case

Table 2.4. *Annual average changes in productivity, 1951-66*

Percentages

Goods industries		Service industries	
Mining	1.6	Transport	2.9
Food, drink and tobacco	1.9	Gas, electricity, water	4.4
Chemicals	4.8	Distribution	2.5
Metals	2.1	Finance	1.3
Engineering	2.5	Professional services	0.4
Textiles	2.8	Miscellaneous services	2.3
Other manufacturing	2.7	Public administration	0.8
Construction	1.6		

SOURCE: A.D. Smith, *The Measurement and Interpretation of Service Output Changes*, London, National Economic Development Office, 1972.

[1] Victor R. Fuchs (ed.), *Production and Productivity in the Service Industries*, New York, Columbia University Press, 1969.

of manufacturing). The initial tax was fairly low and as a proportion of costs could not be said to redress fully the bias against manufactures in the system of indirect taxation. The rate was raised subsequently, before the whole tax was abolished and replaced in 1973 with value-added tax (VAT), which also replaced purchase tax on goods.

Besides securing a broader base for indirect taxation other merits were claimed for selective employment tax. In particular it was suggested that it would offset alleged tendencies to waste labour in some service industries. This question, among others, was exhaustively analysed in two extensive research reports undertaken on behalf of the government by Professor W. B. Reddaway and associates at the Department of Applied Economics in Cambridge. The first report on the distributive trades was published in 1970 and concluded that productivity in the distributive trades had risen significantly more after 1966 than could have been expected on the basis of earlier relationships between employment and the volume of sales in retailing and the pressure of demand for labour. It could not be concluded that the whole of this exceptional rise in productivity was the result of selective employment tax, since at about the same time the abolition of resale price maintenance had come into force and economic reasoning would lead one to expect such a measure to increase the productivity of labour in industries affected. In the final report Professor Reddaway maintained that the evidence was statistically very weak in industries other than distribution, but he personally found 'the evidence for a modest productivity gain moderately persuasive'. These conclusions command fairly general acceptance, though some question has been raised concerning the *scale* of the productivity improvement in distribution which could be attributed to selective employment tax and the abolition of resale price maintenance, it being suggested that certain other factors common to all industries including manufacturing, might also have played a role.

An incidental conclusion of the study, as it referred to the distributive trades, was that the imposition of this particular kind of indirect tax had rather a small effect on gross retail margins (inclusive of tax), thus making selective employment tax an exception to the fairly general rule that a substantial part of indirect taxes is passed on to the final consumer.

3. The Agricultural Sector

Proportionately fewer people are engaged in agriculture in Britain than in any other country of any size − 2.7 per cent of the civil working population − but virtually all suitable land not built upon by towns and cities is in agricultural use, and the sector provides just over a half of the country's food requirements, or nearly 70 per cent of all that can be grown in temperate climates. Britain has been a net importer of food since the middle of the nineteenth century, but the share of home production in total supplies reached a low point between the two wars and has lately been rising a little.

There are about 270,000 farming units in Britain, but of these two-fifths are very small, mostly farmed part-time, and account for less than 6 per cent of the industry's output. Of the 166,000 full-time businesses, 24 per cent are large (employing four or more men) and between them produce more than half the total output. The average size of full-time holdings is 250 acres (101 hectares).

British agriculture is highly specialized and highly capitalized. Three-fifths of full-time farms are devoted to dairying, beef cattle and sheep, a sixth are crop farms and the remainder specialize in pigs, poultry, or horticulture, or they are mixed farms. There is also specialization according to region; for example, arable crops are mainly grown in eastern counties.

The composition of British farm production has not changed a great deal in recent years, as shown in Table 2.5. The principal crops are wheat, barley and potatoes, and the principal livestock products are milk and milk products, which constitute between them over a fifth of total agricultural output.

The total area of land in agricultural use in the early 1960s was the same as in the 1930s, but in the past decade the acreage has diminished by over 5 per cent, partly because of incursions of urban development. Output in real terms is nearly three times that achieved before the war. The proportion of land given to farm crops has risen somewhat, so that the average yield per acre of the principal crops, such as wheat and barley, has about doubled.

More than half of British farms are owned by their occupiers, the remainder being farmed by tenants of private landlords. In the latter cases the capital equipment required to operate the farms is most commonly provided by the tenants. Production methods are highly

Table 2.5. *Distribution of agricultural output,*[a] *1964-5 and 1975-6*

Percentages

	1964-5	*1975-6*
Farm crops	19.9	22.8
Horticulture	11.6	10.4
Livestock	35.7	37.7
Livestock products	32.1	28.4
Total of above	99.3	99.3

SOURCE: CSO, *Annual Abstract of Statistics*, 1977, page 246.
[a] In value terms.

mechanized: there are nearly five tractors to every six people engaged in the industry and, at one tractor to every 33 acres of arable land (13 hectares), Britain has one of the highest tractor-densities in the world.

From the middle of the nineteenth century until the third decade of the present century Britain followed a policy of free trade in goods and services, including food. This meant that, when great advances were made in transport and refrigeration, the British consumer had access to the cheapest food supplies throughout the world. When Britain abandoned free trade in 1932, tariffs were introduced on most imported foodstuffs, with zero or preferential rates for Commonwealth countries. The intention was not primarily to protect British farmers, but to give a trading advantage to exporters in the British colonies and dominions. Since, however, a great many of the preferences were fixed in specific rather than *ad valorem* terms, the value of this concession to Commonwealth suppliers has diminished as prices have risen. Nonetheless, some degree of preference was available to them on 90 to 95 per cent of United Kingdom 1972 imports of food, drink and tobacco, oilseeds and vegetable oils. During the Second World War there was an intensive campaign for the development of British home food supplies and imported supplies came under very close government control, which was gradually relaxed in the postwar period. Since 1 February 1973, Britain has begun to take part in the EEC's Common Agricultural Policy (CAP).

In 1961 two-fifths of British food imports came from Commonwealth countries, a quarter from Western Europe and 13.5 per cent from North America. In the 1960s the Commonwealth share was slowly falling and the West European share rising. Since 1972 the EEC the share has risen strongly (see Table 2.6).

For over half a century the size of the British agricultural industry was largely determined by market forces — by the inability of British farmers to compete with overseas suppliers — but in the First World War and again in the Second overseas supplies were drastically curtailed by submarine warfare. Between the wars a variety of forms of agricultural support were introduced. These were, of course, enormously intensified during the Second World War, and subsequently a higher degree of State support remained than had existed previously. Most industrial countries give State support to agriculture, but in the majority of cases this takes the form of tariffs and/or quantitative restrictions, including outright prohibition of certain imports. Until joining the EEC British policy was quite different. The price paid by British consumers for food in the shops was based on the world price, that is the price of the cheapest import.[1] The British farmer, however, was given a

---

[1] During, and for nearly a decade after, the Second World War, the prices of many foods, whether imported or home produced, were kept

Table 2.6 *Food imports by area of origin, 1972-6*

Percentages

	1972	1974	1975	1976
EEC	31.0	44.0	49.1	44.3
Rest of Western Europe	6.9	6.5	5.2	6.0
North America	11.6	10.9	8.2	10.7
Rest of World	50.5	38.6	37.5	39.0

SOURCE: CSO, *Annual Abstract of Statistics, 1977,* page 320.

guaranteed price for major products other than fruit and vegetables. The difference between this guaranteed price and the market price was made up by a 'deficiency payment' financed by the State. In addition there were specific production grants and subsidies. The guaranteed price and production subsidies were calculated in such a way as to secure for the farmer a reasonable income as well as a surplus to finance the capital requirements of the industry.

Because of the increasing budgetary cost of this system some additional protective measures were introduced in the 1960s designed to reduce the volume of cheap food imports and hence to maintain United Kingdom market prices. The most important were the introduction of minimum import prices and import levies on major cereals and later on beef and veal, negotiation of quotas on pigmeat imports and the introduction of an import duty on mutton and lamb, previously duty-free. Thus, even before joining the EEC, Britain was moving towards a system that was in many respects similar to the CAP, while maintaining the subsidy to farm incomes given via the guaranteed price system and production grants.

The effects of British entry into the EEC in 1973 may be considered from the point of view of farmers, consumers and overseas suppliers. It was generally expected that farmers would be least affected; total farm income rose a fraction more than average between 1972 and 1976. Farmers continue to enjoy protection; competition from other Community members is limited to the extent that there is a common price throughout the area, so that transport costs give natural protection to the local industry; protection from non-Community suppliers is given

down by consumer subsidies. When these were abandoned, various forms of 'agricultural' or production subsidies remained. Consumer food subsidies were re-introduced by the Labour Government of 1974, and in 1974-5 amounted to £854 million. Under the plans contained in the Treasury White Paper of January 1978 (*The Government's Expenditure Plans 1978-79 to 1981-82*, Cmnd 7049 II), they are to be phased out altogether by 1979-80.

by the levies imposed on imports from outside. The exact amount of gain or loss for any particular farmer depends on the type of farming.

For the British consumer it was to be expected that the price of food relative to other products would rise. A 1971 White Paper estimated that by 1978 the retail price of food would be 16 per cent higher than otherwise as a result of joining the EEC.[1] A study made at the Cambridge University Department of Applied Economics put the actual increase by 1978 a little lower — some 12 per cent.[2]

The effect on overseas suppliers is of course to switch towards supplies from other members of the Community and away from previous suppliers. The most notably affected is New Zealand, over a third of whose exports have until lately come to the United Kingdom. The other principal group affected is the cane sugar suppliers covered by the Commonwealth Sugar Agreement.

The farmers producing most commodities are now supported by the CAP. Support prices have been set so high in many cases that surplus 'mountains', for example of butter, or 'lakes', for example of wine, have accumulated. The Cambridge study puts the net direct cost to the United Kingdom balance of payments in 1978 of membership of the EEC at about £1,000 million.

---

[1] Cabinet Office, *The United Kingdom and the European Communities*, Cmnd 4715, London, HMSO, 1971.
[2] *Economic Policy Review*, no. 4, March 1978.

Chapter 3

SOCIAL ISSUES

1. Trade Unions and Labour Relations

Structure and organization

At the end of 1976 the number of workers in the United Kingdom who were members of trade unions was estimated at 12,376,000.[1] This represents 52 per cent of the working population (excluding employers, self-employed and members of the forces). Male membership was 8,816,000 and female membership 3,560,000, so that 61 per cent of male workers and 37 per cent of female were members of unions. The number of unions operating in the United Kingdom was estimated at 462 in 1976 and this total has shown a steady decline over the years, from 630 in 1965 and from 688 in 1955.[2] Total membership was 7,875,000.[3] The rising number of members coupled with the falling number of unions has meant an increase in their average size. This has occurred both through internal growth and through amalgamations. The largest unions in the United Kingdom at present are the Transport and General Workers Union with a 1977 membership of 1,929,834, the Amalgamated Union of Engineering Workers with 1,412,076 and the General and Municipal Workers Union with 916,438.[4]

The great majority of unions in the United Kingdom are affiliated to the Trades Union Congress (TUC), which has its headquarters in London. In 1977 the TUC had an affiliated membership of 11,515,920. Similar bodies exist in Northern Ireland and Scotland, but many unions which represent members in these areas are in any case affiliated to the TUC.

Unions in the United Kingdom have developed in the main along craft lines, except in the case of general unions which recruit from a

---

[1] *Department of Employment Gazette*, November 1977.

[2] The 1976 figure is for organizations defined as trade unions in the Trade Unions and Labour Relations Act, 1974; it excludes 31 organizations previously regarded as trade unions by the Department of Employment.

[3] Department of Employment, *British Labour Statistics: historical abstract 1886-1968*, London, HMSO, 1971.

[4] TUC, *Report of the 109th Annual Congress, 1977*, Blackpool.

wide variety of workers. Craft unions are those to which workers with a particular skill, craft or training belong, regardless of the industry in which they are employed; electricians in all industries will tend to be in one union, as will engineers. Whereas general unions have usually catered for less skilled occupations, craft unions predominate in trades or professions requiring significant levels of skill and/or training. This form of union organization along craft lines contrasts with the industrial union, under which workers of many different skills will be in a single union relevant to the industry in which they are employed. Industrial unions are common in some European countries, for example West Germany. They are not found in the United Kingdom, although in the mining industry the National Union of Mineworkers comes close to the pattern, representing as it does the industrial interests of the vast majority of workers in the industry. More usually the role of bargaining agent at the industry level is filled by a confederation of trade unions. In construction, for example, there is the National Federation of Building Trades Operatives, which operates at industry level.

Unions in the United Kingdom are normally governed by an executive council, which is elected from and by the membership of the union, either directly or through an annual delegate conference. The majority of unions have a full-time staff headed by a General Secretary, who is the national spokesman for the union and its main administrator. Most sizeable unions also appoint full-time paid local officials to deal with union business at a local level. In almost all cases unions have an organization of lay members at local and regional level. Union members as a rule belong to a group at their place of work, but are also likely to be members of a union branch in the geographical location of their work — a branch which includes members from other work-places in the area. The union group in the work-place usually elects a spokesman, often called a shop steward. Where there are several unions involved in an establishment, there is commonly a committee consisting of shop stewards from each union, and this body is frequently an important negotiating agent with management.

Trade union objectives

Trade unions exist to act in the interest of their members; in general this has been seen in practice in terms of maintaining and improving the terms and conditions of employment for various groups within the union, although unions frequently assist individual members in cases such as claims for industrial injuries compensation and claims alleging unfair dismissal. Apart from these individual cases, some of the more important matters on which unions negotiate include pay, hours of work, working conditions, industrial health and safety, fringe benefits, pensions and redundancy arrangements. Popularly, pay is perhaps the most obvious single concern of union members, and the role of unions is sometimes discussed solely in relation to pay, but other matters pursued by unions in attempting to improve their members' terms and conditions of employment are of considerable importance and should not be overlooked.

The organization of workers into craft unions has implications for collective bargaining on many of the issues mentioned in the previous paragraph, because unions will often seek to negotiate national agreements which set minimum standards for rates of pay, hours of work, holidays, overtime and other premium payments, recruitment and apprenticeship. These minimum standards provide a base, and workers at the plant or company level can then negotiate individual additions to the agreed national minima. This may lead to differences between rates of pay at the place of work and those agreed nationally.

In pursuit of their various objectives, unions are often parties to procedures which have been agreed with management to regulate the conduct of negotiations or the settlement of a grievance. In the event of negotiations being unsuccessful the union may resort to direct action in support of its case. Direct action can vary through several types of non-cooperation to a complete withdrawal of labour – a strike. Industrial action may occur before all procedures have been exhausted and may be undertaken by a particular group of local union members without prior permission of the executive council of their union or unions. If action continues without such sanction it is called unofficial. Action which has been approved by the national union organization, or which has started and subsequently received such backing, is termed official action. Many unions pay strike pay to members engaged in official withdrawals of labour.

Trade unions and the government

Trade unions, employers' associations and the general field of labour relations are the responsibility of the Department of Employment, formerly the Ministry of Labour. Before the 1960s the role of the Ministry of Labour was to assist in the orderly running of the system of industrial relations in the United Kingdom, with little reference to or interest in the subject or outcome of particular disputes. For many years the Ministry offered facilities for conciliation and arbitration in the event of a dispute and the Minister had the power to establish a Court of Inquiry into a particular dispute if it was considered necessary.

This form of *ad hoc* arrangement was, in the main, satisfactory as long as unions and employers were engaged in a process of free collective bargaining at either national or local level. In the 1960s, however, increasing government concern with inflation and the subsequent development of incomes policies, wage restraint and other anti-inflation instruments has meant that the government is no longer content to leave unions and employers to negotiate freely. The government is now more interested and involved in the outcome of collectively bargained decisions and much more concerned with industrial disputes in the course of such bargaining. The government, central and local, is a very large employer in its own right, and this provides another incentive for its growing involvement with industrial relations.

As a consequence, the trade union movement, through the TUC, and the main employers, through the Confederation of British Industry (CBI), are now frequently consulted by governments on the formulation of policies, particularly those concerned with inflation. Representatives of both bodies sit on the National Economic Development Council, which is chaired by the Chancellor of the Exchequer. The Conservative government in 1972 consulted extensively with both bodies in the formulation of its counter-inflation policy, and the Labour government which assumed office in 1974 made their understanding with the TUC, the 'social contract', an important feature of their economic strategy. Consultation with the TUC and the CBI took place before the government introduced from July 1975 a twelve-month limit on wage rises of £6 a week, and before a second stage of wage restraint was introduced from the following July.

Trade unions and the law

Apart from consultation over policy, governments in recent years have been closely involved with changes in the legal framework regulating trade union conduct and organization. In 1964 a Royal Commission was set up under Lord Donovan to review the current state of trade unions and employers' organizations; the Labour government received its report in 1968[1]. Although the Labour Party traditionally has been closely linked to the trade union movement and has drawn much support from it, in the aftermath of the report the government introduced proposals for legislation to curb what was seen as a major problem of unofficial or unconstitutional strikes.[2] The action proposed was stronger than that recommended by the report and the TUC was strongly opposed to the penal sanctions contained in the proposals. The government subsequently abandoned their attempts to legislate, relying instead on the TUC's undertaking to implement a programme of action giving Congress more power to involve themselves in unofficial strikes

---

[1] Royal Commission on Trade Unions and Employers' Associations, *Report*, Cmnd 3623, London, HMSO, 1968.

[2] Department of Employment and Productivity, *In Place of Strife: a policy for industrial relations*, Cmnd 3888, London, HMSO, 1969.

and inter-union disputes. The other move following the Donovan Report was the establishment of a standing Commission on Industrial Relations (CIR), which was to examine problems concerning recognition by employers of trade unions and other industrial relations issues.

The Conservative government which came into office in 1970 passed in 1971 a wide-ranging Industrial Relations Act. This established a new branch of the High Court, the National Industrial Relations Court (NIRC). The Court was empowered to sit in judgement over what were called cases of 'unfair industrial practices' if one of the parties brought a case and could impose fines if breaches of the law occurred. The NIRC could also impose a full ballot of union members, or a 'cooling-off' period to postpone a planned industrial action if the government made an application.

The opposition of the trade union movement and the Labour Party to the Industrial Relations Act led to considerable controversy over the decisions of the NIRC and, when Labour was elected to office in February 1974, repeal of the Industrial Relations Act was given high priority. The Trade Union and Labour Relations Act 1974 abolished the NIRC and the CIR, and in general restored the situation broadly to a pre-1971 state, although retaining greater protection against unfair dismissal.

Further employment measures were enacted or came into force during 1975. The Equal Pay Act 1970 became operative in December 1975, having given employers a transitional period of five years to meet its requirements. The Sex Discrimination Act 1975 makes illegal discrimination on grounds of sex or marriage in many fields including employment and training. The Employment Protection Act 1975 extends the rights of employees regarding unfair dismissal and discrimination short of dismissal because of union membership. It institutes new procedures for handling redundancy situations and provides in certain circumstances for guarantees of pay by an employer when he is unable to provide work for reasons other than a trade dispute.

The Act also established on a statutory basis the Advisory, Conciliation and Arbitration Service (ACAS), which was first set up in September 1974. ACAS has taken over and extended the role previously filled by the Department of Employment in providing conciliation in industrial disputes and union recognition problems, arbitration and mediation. The emphasis is on a voluntary solution to industrial relations problems and ACAS has to be approached by at least one of the parties to a dispute before becoming involved, although it can inquire into any situation and offer advice independently. The body is independent of government and controlled by a representative council.

2. Social Policy

For at least a century there has been a secular trend for a higher proportion of both national resources and public expenditure to be devoted to social services. Even before the First World War, the idea was emerging that social services should not be regarded as a form of charity, but rather as one of the natural benefits available to the citizens of a civilized State. Stimulated by both world wars, the State increased its powers and pushed ahead with the development of social services. But it was not until after the Second World War that the services became comprehensive. The broad pattern of the social services as they are at present was laid down in the 1940s, but they have not remained static, and developments in the last thirty years have aimed at continued improvement in the levels of services and more satisfactory administration to cope with rising needs. Table 3.1 shows public expenditure on the social services and housing in recent years as a percentage of gross national product at market prices.

Health and personal social services

The National Health Service was set up in 1948 to promote the provision of comprehensive health treatment available according to medical need without regard to any insurance qualification. It was originally free to users, but various charges have subsequently been introduced from time to time. The aim of policy has been to meet needs for cure and rehabilitation, to prevent illness and to promote health. The methods by which these aims were pursued have been an increase in personnel, better training and research, greater integration of services, and the renewal and modernization of the hospitals.

Between 1951 and 1976 the medical and nursing staff in the hospitals more than doubled, and other professional and technical staff more than trebled. The number of general medical practitioners increased much more slowly — by only about 30 per cent over the same period — while the number of dentists rose by about a quarter.

The trend in health administration, particularly over the last decade, has been towards greater integration of the services provided by hospitals, general practitioners and local authorities. This has been particularly evident in the treatment of children, the elderly, the mentally ill and the mentally handicapped. There has been increased emphasis on rehabilitation to reduce the length of stay in hospital and to return patients to their own homes as soon as possible, with continued treatment when at out-patient clinics or in day-hospitals. As a result, the average length of stay in hospitals generally has decreased sharply, at the same time as the number of patients treated both as in-patients and as out-patients has risen rapidly. Moreover, much of the treatment is in more modern hospitals as, in the 1960s and 1970s, the government embarked on a programme of rehabilitation and, where necessary, rebuilding.

Table 3.1 *Public expenditure*[a] *on the social services and housing (at current prices), 1951-77*

	1951	1961	1971	1977
		(£ millions)		
Education	433	1,012	3,058	8,307
Health and personal social	564	1,088	2,559	7,996
Social security benefits	707	1,628	4,308	13,213
Housing	367	555	1,310	5,111
Total	2,071	4,283	11,235	34,627
		(percentages)		
As a proportion of GNP[b]	14.4	15.6	19.5	24.6

SOURCE: CSO, *National Income and Expenditure* (various issues).
[a]Current and capital expenditure and grants by public authorities and public corporations.
[b]At market prices.

Although there are only indirect indicators of progress in health services, they suggest striking improvements in standards of physical health in the last twenty years. The main infectious diseases, which were once the major cause of death of people of working age, have been virtually eliminated as health problems. People in Britain live longer than in most other countries; mortality continues to fall; the proportion of children who die in the first year of life is among the lowest of all countries in the world, although higher than in Japan and France. There has been a steady increase in sickness and death from degenerative diseases, largely attributable to the ageing of the population. Part of the increased cost of the health service is due to changes in the age structure (particularly to a higher proportion of people of pensionable age, who make heavier demands on the service), but a major part is due to technological changes – the use of new drugs, new diagnostic tests and new treatment in virtually every field of medicine.

Education
Between 1951 and 1977 public expenditure on education at constant prices increased about three and a half times. As a proportion of GNP it has risen from 3.4 per cent in 1951 to 6.7 per cent in 1977. This reflects a considerable increase in the numbers in full-time education, both at schools and at universities and colleges of further education. The growth has been uneven, reflecting the fluctuating birth rates since the war. Between 1971 and 1976 the number of children under 15 fell by 4.3 per cent; this has already affected the demand for primary education and the numbers in secondary education will begin to fall in the early 1980s.

The school-leaving age was raised to 15 in 1947 and to 16 in 1973. In addition a decreasing proportion of pupils leave school at the first opportunity; instead they stay on voluntarily. As a result, by 1976 there were over 50 per cent more pupils at school than in 1951. The increase in the number of children has been more than proportionately matched by increased numbers of teachers. In the public sector, where more than 90 per cent of all children receive their education, many more pupils are now taught in comprehensive schools. There has been a massive school building programme in the last thirty years and, although there are still a number of unsatisfactory schools, particularly in urban areas, a large proportion of children are now educated in modern schools.

The increase in numbers of pupils staying on at school has also been reflected in an improvement in standards in the school-leaving examinations and an increasing proportion of school leavers now move into full-time further education.

A ten-year education programme was announced by the government in December 1972. The proposals involved substantially increased expenditure in five sectors; a new programme of nursery education; a larger building programme for the renewal of secondary and special as well as primary schools; a larger teaching force to improve further the staffing standards in schools; new measures to improve the pre-service and in-service training of teachers; and the development in higher education of a wider range of opportunities for both students and institutions.

Income support

The system of income support consists of many elements, but the central one is the social security system. Social security payments increased from 5.5 per cent of personal income in 1951 to 12.0 per cent in 1977. More than half of this increase was due to higher expenditure on retirement pensions.

The main purposes of the social security system are to replace earnings in periods of interruption or cessation of earnings, and to transfer extra income to those who currently have family responsibilities. This involves a redistribution between those in good health and the sick, between the working population and the unemployed and retired, and between those currently with family responsibilities and those without.

The postwar National Insurance scheme created rights to benefits which are taking years to mature, before the whole population over pension age can draw pensions earned by contributions under the scheme, or all widows, long-term sick and work-injured can receive benefits on the new basis. Thus the cost of social security has been increasing because the postwar scheme is still maturing. In addition, a number of changes in policy since it was introduced, such as the family income supplement, have added to the cost. Under a new State pension scheme introduced in April 1978, retirement, invalidity and widows' pensions became earnings-related and protected against inflation.

Between 1951 and 1977 total expenditure on retirement pensions at constant prices increased more than fivefold, although the population of pension ages increased by only 44 per cent. But the proportion of the population of pension age actually receiving pensions increased from 60 per cent in 1951 to 90 per cent in 1976. This is mainly because a higher proportion of pensioners had had time to pay contributions from 1948 onwards which gave them title to pensions, but there has also been a trend towards earlier retirement.

The rates of both absence through sickness and unemployment are also higher now than in the 1950s. A large increase in sickness absence in the 1960s was almost entirely due to increases in incapacity rates at all ages, but the numbers claiming sickness benefit seem to have levelled off in the 1970s. The reasons for these trends are complex and they are not confined to Britain.

Between 1951 and 1977 the population under 21 increased by over 20 per cent, but children for whom family allowances were paid increased more — by 36 per cent. This was partly because the number of families with two or more dependent children increased more than the number of children, and partly because an increasing number of children stayed on at school after the age of 15 and continued to be counted for purposes of family allowances.

For all these reasons social security expenditure has been increasing within the framework of the 1945-6 legislation quite apart from changes in policy. In addition benefits have been increased, not just in line with changes in prices, but with the object of improving their real value. Improvements have taken the form of supplements related to earnings and increases in the real value of basic flat-rate benefits and allowances. A further policy aim has been to ensure that those entitled to benefits and allowances actually claim them.

A further part of income support is the supplementary benefits scheme, which in 1966 succeeded national assistance. Every person aged 16 or over who is not in full-time work, attending school or involved in a pay dispute and whose resources are insufficient to meet his requirements is entitled to a supplementary benefit. In 1948 11.5 per cent of persons over pension age were drawing national assistance; in 1976 17 per cent were drawing supplementary benefits.

Housing

Satisfactory housing implies adequate numbers of dwellings of the right size and quality in the right places. There are over 20 million dwellings in Britain and nationally the numbers of households and dwellings are about equal, but they are unevenly distributed and housing shortages persist in the more prosperous commercial and industrial centres, such as London and Birmingham.

Over 9 million new dwellings have been built in Britain since 1945 and more than two families in five now live in a postwar dwelling. During the past thirty years the demolition of slum dwellings and higher standards for new housebuilding have led to significant improvements in the general quality of British housing. However, there remain a large number of older dwellings, some of which have been kept in good repair and modernized, while many others are unsatisfactory by modern standards. A sample survey in 1971 showed that 12 per cent of dwellings lacked an internal water closet and 7 per cent were regarded as unfit.

The number of people owning their own homes has increased rapidly in the last fifty years, until over half of all dwellings are owned by their occupiers. Some 30 per cent are rented from public housing authorities and most of the remainder are rented from private landlords. A national system of rent rebate and allowance schemes has been introduced to assist poorer tenants. The main objectives of government housing policy are to secure a decent home for every family at a price within its means and to ensure fairness between one citizen and another in giving and receiving help towards housing costs. Government subsidies are available for local authorities which incur financial debts in clearing slums and providing adequate public sector housing in areas of housing shortage. Another major objective has been to enable more people with moderate means to become owner-occupiers. The government has been concerned to ensure that the best use is made of the existing housing stock and particular emphasis is placed on renewal rather than clearance.

Nevertheless, a satisfactory housing policy has proved difficult to achieve. Rent control has led to many anomalies and the rapid move to owner-occupation has caused big increases in house prices and a shortage of mortgage funds. Moreover, sharp changes in policy have resulted from changes in governments and there have been wide variations in the resources devoted to housing investment. A housing policy which will achieve the objectives described above has yet to be evolved.

Chapter 4

PUBLIC FINANCE AND NATIONALIZED INDUSTRIES

1. The Management of Public Expenditure

Although adjustments to the level of public expenditure have never usurped the role of taxation changes as the principal means of short-term economic regulation, it is difficult to over-estimate the significance of public sector demand both to the growth and full utilization of resources in the long term, and to the short-term stabilization of demand. Since 1961, with the publication of the Plowden Report on the *Control of Public Expenditure*, it has been an established axiom of policy that the growth of public sector demand in aggregate should be decided by reference to the 'prospective development of income and economic resources', the measure of which is taken as the secular growth-rate of GDP. Under this system, the objective of policy is to balance public sector and other claims on resources (consumption, private investment and exports) in the medium term (of five years), so that the need for short-term interventions is minimized, both with respect to the necessity for correcting destabilizing fluctuations in public expenditure itself, and with respect to counter-cyclical demand operations. Because of the high degree of inflexibility in public programmes such interventions can prove costly. However, although this strategy has always allowed for modest changes in public spending where cyclical conditions warrant it, calls made on the instrument have tended to increase. Since 1973-4 changes in expenditure plans have been much larger than previously envisaged.

Since the establishment of the Public Expenditure Survey Committee in 1961, public expenditure has been managed by means of annual reviews of expenditure plans for three to five years ahead. From 1961 to 1967 public expenditure plans were framed around the National Economic Development Council and the National Plan growth exercises. The annual public expenditure White Papers, which have been published regularly since 1969, have been prepared against less optimistic projections of available resources, though with changing ideas of the proportion of such resources which the public sector should pre-empt.

If public expenditure is to maintain a given share of national resources, it must grow at the same rate as the productive capacity of the economy in the longer run. The strategy of planning public spending by reference to annual average growth-rates over a period of five years has, however, frequently run into difficulties. Not only has the oil crisis made the longer-run growth-rate of the economy more uncertain than previously, but the control of spending programmes has appeared to break down from time to time. As can be seen from Table 4.1, the medium-term growth-rates written into the annual expenditure plans since 1968 have tended to fall some way below the 3 per cent per annum accepted as a guideline up to 1974. However, the growth of total public expenditure in volume terms was still 2¾ per cent per annum between 1968-9 and 1978-9, as opposed to a GDP growth of under 2 per cent per annum. There are a number of reasons for this apparent failure to plan public expenditure effectively, not least being the calls of reflationary counter-cyclical policy mentioned above.[1]

It has also to be remembered that the cost of providing public services rises faster, over a period of years, than the amount of services provided. This is because output increases in the government sector only when extra manpower is recruited; the productivity of existing employees is taken as fixed. (In fact, no attempt is made to measure changes in the output of public employees in Britain.) When, as happens in the longer run, public employees demand real wage increases parallel with those in the enterprise sector of the economy (where wage increases are not fully reflected in prices because of productivity increases), public output will increase in cost relative to other goods (the so-called 'relative price effect'). Public spending therefore increases by

Table 4.1   *Planned and actual growth-rates of public expenditure,*[a]
1968-9 to 1978-9
                                        Percentages per annum

	Volume	*Cost*
Planned[b] in Surveys for:		
1968-9	2.8	3.0
1970-2	2.2	2.5
1974	1.4	1.4
1975	1.0	1.2
1976	0.4	0.2
1977	2.5	2.5
Actual, 1968-9 to 1978-9	2.75	3.15

SOURCE: Public Expenditure White Papers (various years).
[a] Includes investment in nationalized industries, but excludes (for the sake of continuity) investment grants and child benefits.
[b] Annual averages for four years ahead.

---

[1] For a discussion of the causes of public expenditure excesses and shortfalls see R.W.R. Price, 'Public expenditure' in F.T. Blackaby (ed.), *British Economic Policy, 1960-74,* Cambridge University Press, 1978, pp. 128-31.

this amount *and* the growth in output volume. This composite growth-rate is shown in the second column of Table 4.1; as the cost of public spending grew on average 0.4 per cent per annum faster than its volume over the years 1968-9 to 1978-9, the annual average growth-rate of the cost was 3.15 per cent per annum.[1]

In practice the relative price effect does not occur uniformly from year to year. In some years public pay falls behind private; in others it catches up, as in 1974-5. The experience of this year, when there was a large unforecast relative price change, persuaded the Treasury to introduce a system of cash limits, and these have been central to the control of central and local government spending since 1975.

2. Changing Patterns of Public Expenditure

The above growth-rates imply that public spending has increased its share of domestic resources, and Table 4.2 analyses the extent of this by expressing total expenditure and its components as ratios of GNP at market prices. (This measure incorporates changes due to relative price changes; shares in national *output* would increase rather more slowly.)

The expenditure breakdown is confined to the central and local governments, but the (mainly capital) expenditure of the public corporations is added to the table, together with net lending, in order to indicate the total size of the public sector as it is defined in the national accounts.[2] The table also categorizes expenditure on an economic basis, distinguishing current from capital expenditures, and direct expenditures on goods and services from transfers, in the form of subsidies and grants to the personal and overseas sectors, and from interest payments in respect of the national debt. Expenditures are also subdivided on a functional basis, distinguishing them by main head of programme.

Because public expenditure is made up of quite heterogenous elements — goods and services, transfers, loans, land purchases, etc. — there are difficulties in interpreting the ratios shown as *shares* of total national productive resources. However, if we reduce the various spending components to their 'factor cost' content by netting out indirect taxes, purchases of land, etc., we obtain the resource shares given at the foot of Table 4.2 — perhaps the best measures of the relative size of the public sector's demand on resources, both directly, through purchases

---

[1] This growth-rate includes the effects of *relative* price changes only; the growth-rate including *general* changes in the price level would, of course, be far higher.

[2] As from 1976-7 investment by the nationalized industries is included in the White Paper definition of public spending only if it is financed by government loans.

Table 4.2. *Public expenditure in the United Kingdom as a proportion of GNP at market prices, 1960-77*

Percentages

	1960	1965	1970	1975	1977
General government expenditure[a]					
Goods and services					
Consumption	16.3	16.6	17.4	22.1	20.6
Capital formation	3.3	4.2	4.8	4.9	3.5
Total	19.6	20.8	22.2	27.0	24.1
Transfers	8.7	9.8	12.0	15.0	15.0
Debt interest	4.0	3.7	3.9	4.0	4.6
Expenditure, excluding debt interest, by function					
Defence	6.2	5.8	4.7	5.0	4.8
Social services excluding education	9.6	10.8	12.3	15.0	15.4
Education	3.5	4.4	4.9	6.3	5.6
Housing	1.6	2.0	2.5	4.2	3.6
Other	7.4	7.6	9.8	11.5	9.7
Total expenditure, excluding debt interest, by spending authority					
Central government					
Goods and services	12.0	11.5	11.7	14.0	13.2
Transfers	8.1	9.3	11.4	14.0	14.0
Total	20.1	20.8	23.1	28.0	27.2
Local authorities					
Goods and services	7.6	9.3	10.5	13.0	10.9
Transfers	0.6	0.5	0.6	1.0	1.0
Total	8.2	9.8	11.1	14.0	11.9
Total public authorities' expenditure[a]					
Excluding debt interest	28.4	30.6	34.2	42.0	39.1
Including debt interest	32.3	34.3	38.1	46.0	43.8
Public corporations' expenditure[ab]	3.5	3.8	3.5	5.0	3.8
Net lending	0.5	0.9	0.5	1.8	0.1
Total public sector expenditure	36.3	39.0	42.1	52.8	47.7
Total public sector resource share[c]	34.9	38.1	40.8	49.2	45.0
of which:					
Direct claims	24.6	26.7	28.1	32.6	30.5
Indirect claims	10.3	11.4	12.7	16.6	14.5

SOURCES: CSO, *National Income and Expenditure* (various issues); NIESR estimates.

  [a]Excluding net lending.
  [b]Net of transactions with the government.
  [c]Equivalent to demand on national output, as defined, for instance, in Treasury, *Public Expenditure to 1979-80*, Table 4.2. On this definition expenditure is net of (i) investment grants, (ii) imputed rents, (iii) indirect taxes on public sector transactions and intra-sector subsidies, (iv) direct taxes on transfers and debt interest, (v) net lending and net purchases of land and existing buildings and (vi) the estimated savings by the recipients of transfers and debt interest. The denominator is taken here as GDP at *factor cost*.

of current production, and indirectly, through transfers of purchasing power.[1]

In the latter half of the 1950s and the early 1960s public expenditure was a relatively stable proportion of GNP, but since 1962 it has been characterized by fairly substantial relative rates of growth. From 1952 the room for the growth of social and welfare expenditure, the expanding elements in GNP, was provided by the decline in defence expenditure and by a preference for private rather than public dwellings investment. With the assumption of high growth targets from the end of 1962, however, public expenditure embarked on a significant expansion, which raised its share of GNP substantially, partly because public demand achieved the targets set for it while the other components of demand and GNP as a whole did not. The peak of the public sector expansion in the 1960s was reached in 1967, before devaluation, when its resource share was about 41.5 per cent; there was a pause for a few years after that, but expansion resumed in 1972, with the pre-oil crisis reflation. The peak years for expansion, however, were the two immediately following the oil crisis, when there was some criticism that the system of control had broken down. Partly because GNP itself failed to grow in these years, partly because public spending rose rapidly, the resource share taken by the public sector increased to nearly 50 per cent. The cut-backs announced in late 1975 and 1976 succeeded in bringing public spending back to more substainable, though still historically high, proportions.

Nearly all sectors of public demand have shared in this overall expansion, though some programmes have been more consistent than others. Housing investment, for instance, underwent a particularly strong expansion between 1962 and 1967, and then suffered an almost equally strong reaction until 1972. The priority given to this sector in the last years of the period, together with the large increases in housing subsidies in 1974, temporarily restored its position as the fastest growing element over the period as a whole. Education, on the other hand, was the most consistently fastest growing sector until it began to lose impetus from 1972 with inflation and revised ideas about future needs. The National Health Service has also demanded an increasing share of resources, while the opposite is true of defence, which actually underwent a decline in volume terms, as well as a drastic fall in its share of total expenditures.

A corollary of all this has been that the local authority sector, which, although it does not necessarily initiate the policies, is responsible for most expenditure on housing and education, has expanded faster than the central government sector as far as goods and services

---

[1] See footnote c to Table 4.2. A fuller definition of this concept may be found in Treasury, *Public Expenditure White Papers: handbook on methodology*, London, HMSO, 1972, Chapter V.

are concerned. Until the housing upsurge of 1973-4 this has been expressed more in current than capital expenditures. Central government investment on such projects as roads, hospitals and industrial regeneration was itself extremely buoyant up to 1973, and one has also to remember that local authority environmental investment was, from July 1965 to the end of the 1960s, a favourite target for short-term cuts.

On central government account, also, there have been a number of fast-expanding programmes based on transfer payments, only a small element of which is administered locally. From 1960 to 1977 the share of transfers in GNP increased from 8.7 per cent to 15.0 per cent, with the increases concentrated particularly on the years 1965 to 1968, and on the period 1972 to 1974; in 1974 alone the share rose by 2 percentage points. The expansion of the transfer element in public expenditures can be traced to reasons of both social and economic policy, with social security benefits representing the means of redistributing income and the medium of reflation, as in the period 1972-4. Subsidies combine both these uses with the further one of combating inflation. The remarkable rise in subsidies between 1972 and 1974 began with compensation for price restraint in the nationalized industries, and was followed, in 1974, by large increases in food and housing subsidies.

Indirect claims on national resources have increased proportionally faster than direct ones, although they account about equally for the 9½ per cent increase in the total resource share (from 35 to 45 per cent of GNP) between 1960 and 1977. It is also noteworthy that the drop in investment since the oil crisis has meant that the increase has recently been more in current than in capital spending, though this was not the case up to 1973.

3. Taxation

In some respects the United Kingdom appears to be a relatively highly taxed country. In the 1970s the ratio of tax revenues to GNP has been, on average, just over 30 per cent and, though this is not markedly different from the European average, it is somewhat high considering that Britain has a relatively low income per head. There is evidence, as can be seen in chart 4.1, that the tax—GNP ratio increases as countries grow more wealthy. The diagonal line shows the extent of this, and it can be seen that, given the United Kingdom's below average income per head, one might anticipate a below-average, rather than average, ratio of tax to GNP.

However, other countries rely on National Insurance Contributions for revenue more than us. Since these have characteristics akin to taxation, a fuller picture of deductions from personal income is given by adding these to tax revenues proper. It then appears (part B of the chart) that the United Kingdom is relatively lightly taxed compared to the European average of just over 40 per cent; in 1975 the tax plus contributions ratio of the United Kingdom was 37 per cent, as opposed to the 39 per cent one might expect given its relative income per head. The most striking differences lie in the composition of government revenues rather than the actual amount taken from private incomes. In particular, Britain places considerable emphasis on personal income taxation relative to expenditure taxation, and raises relatively little through social security contributions.

Chart 4.1 *International comparison of tax burdens, 1975*

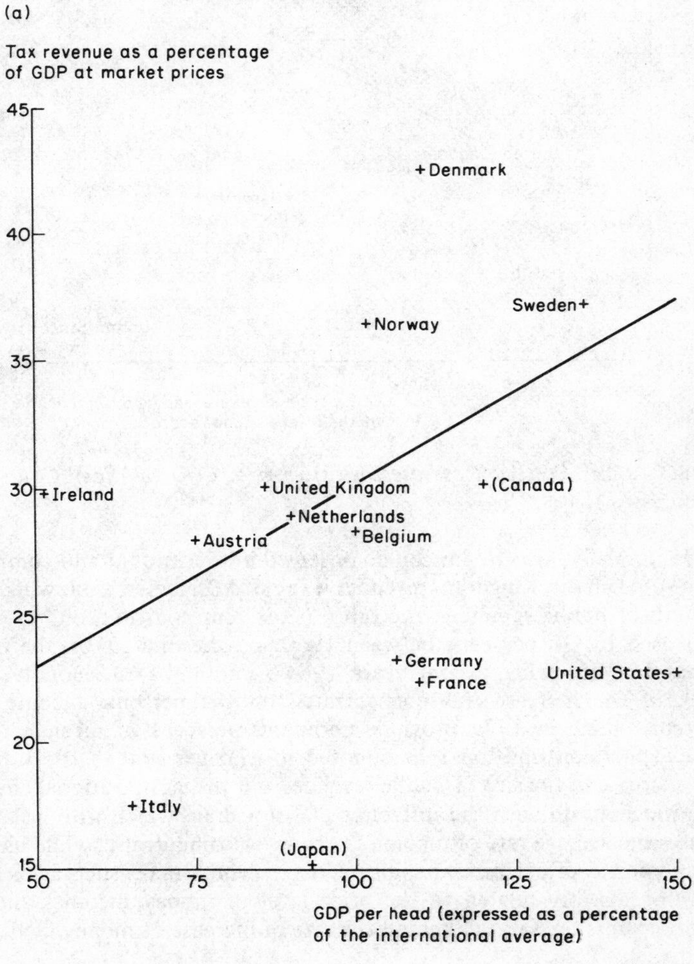

(a)

Tax revenue as a percentage
of GDP at market prices

GDP per head (expressed as a percentage
of the international average)

(b)

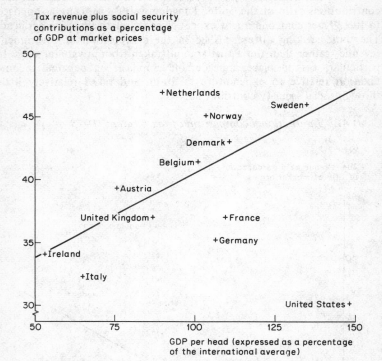

Tax revenue plus social security contributions as a percentage of GDP at market prices

GDP per head (expressed as a percentage of the international average)

SOURCE: OECD, *Revenue Statistics of OECD Member Countries 1965-1975*, Paris, 1977.

Historically, two trends can be observed in the amount and composition of United Kingdom revenues (Table 4.3). First, following the growth of public spending, the ratio of tax plus contributions to GNP increased by 30 per cent between 1960 and the mid-1970s, the main expansion occurring in the years 1964-9 and 1974-6. Secondly, the bulk of the increase was concentrated on the personal income tax system, which in 1975 provided about 40 per cent of revenue from taxes (plus contributions), as opposed to 27½ per cent in 1960. Both the increase in the size of public revenues and the compositional change had much to do with the influence of fiscal drag, which with inflation causes the average rate of income tax to rise automatically, while having the opposite effect on expenditure tax receipts; taxes such as excises are not directly related to the price level or money incomes and so their receipts tend to fall behind the rate of increase of money GNP.

The history of expenditure taxation has been the opposite of that of the income tax. Budgetary increases in tax rates have frequently had to be brought in to compensate for the decreases in real yield which are caused by inflation. On the other hand, the tendency for the effective rate of income tax to increase automatically has, in the past, given Chancellors the leeway to make income tax cuts which were more apparent than real, or allowed them to increase tax rates without overtly doing so. Since 1977 this situation no longer exists, because personal allowances must be increased in line with inflation unless Parliament explicitly agrees otherwise.

Because of the active use of deficit finance in economic management, total expenditures are rarely matched by revenues. The difference

Table 4.3. *Tax revenue in the United Kingdom as a proportion of GNP at market prices, 1960-77*

Percentages

	1960	1965	1970	1975	1977
Taxes on income	10.6	11.1	14.4	16.0	14.4
Personal incomes	7.7	9.1	11.3	14.6[a]	13.0[a]
Company incomes[b]	2.9	2.0	3.1	1.4[a]	1.4[a]
Taxes on expenditure	13.1	13.8	16.4	13.6	14.5
Central government	10.1	10.4	12.8	9.8	10.8
Local authorities (rates)	3.0	3.4	3.6	3.8	3.7
Taxes on capital	0.9	0.8	1.3	0.8	0.7
Social security contributions	3.5	4.7	5.1	6.6	6.7
Total tax revenue					
Excluding social security	24.6	25.7	32.1	30.4	29.6
Including social security	28.1	30.4	37.2	37.0	36.3
Other public sector revenue[c]	5.4	5.2	4.9	5.7	7.2
Total public sector revenue[c]	33.5	35.6	42.1	42.7	43.5
Borrowing requirement	2.8	3.4	—	10.1	4.2
Total expenditure (Table 4.2)	36.3	39.0	42.1	52.8	47.7

SOURCE: CSO, *National Income and Expenditure* (various issues).

[a] Personal income tax includes, and company tax excludes, tax credits charged as advance corporation tax.

[b] Including foreign-owned companies.

[c] Including non-trading capital consumption, rent dividends and interest, and gross trading surpluses of the central government and public corporations.

is the 'borrowing requirement', which varies from year to year with economic circumstances. It reached a peak in 1975, when it was just over 10 per cent of GNP.

4. Reforming the Tax Structure

In addition to the predominant role in counter-cyclical policy and demand management played by the tax system (particularly through changes in investment incentives, in personal income tax rates and allowances, and in the rates of indirect taxes governed by the regulator) the period has witnessed a series of major structural reforms. These were designed for a variety of secular objectives: to simplify the tax structure, to increase capacity and channel resources to more productive uses, to encourage growth and investment, to attain a more equal distribution of resources and other social objectives and, more recently, to co-ordinate United Kingdom fiscal structures and practices more closely with those of other EEC members. The following is a summary of the most significant of these changes.

Corporate taxation

Three major phases in the pattern of corporate taxation may be distinguished during the period. First, from 1958 to 1965 companies were subject to both a uniform profits tax and, in addition, income tax at the standard rate – chargeable on both retained and distributed profits. However, the income tax on distributions was treated as a withholding tax, creditable by the shareholder against the tax liability on his dividend income. In 1965 the uniform profits tax was renamed the corporation tax and the rate increased from 15 to 40 per cent, while, to encourage companies to 'plough back profits for expansion', the income tax on retentions was abolished. Finally, in 1973, after considerable debate about whether the pre-1965 system should be re-established, a new system based on the French 'imputation' method was introduced, under which a single rate of corporation tax was maintained, but the additional layer of income tax on distributions was abolished. Instead, companies paying a distribution become liable to an advance payment of corporation tax and the shareholder is imputed with a corresponding tax credit, which is sufficient exactly to offset his charge to income tax at the basic rate. The main argument for the 1973 reform, namely that, by removing the discrimination against distributions, greater freedom of capital movements both domestically and across international frontiers would be achieved, is reflected in the decision of the EEC Commission that the British imputation method should become the model for company taxation in the Community.

To encourage productive investment, successive governments have introduced a multiplicity of measures designed to provide financial incentives for fixed investment. For most of the period incentives were provided through capital allowances designed to provide relief from tax in respect of outlays on plant and machinery, industrial buildings and certain other qualifying capital assets; a system of accelerated depreciation operated through a combination of initial (first-year) and investment allowances, which varied both regionally and for different types of asset. Between 1966 and 1970, however, a system of cash grants to manufacturing, construction and extractive industries replaced the investment and initial allowances. The reversal of the grants policy in 1970 led to a rationalization and simplification of the pre-1966 system of accelerated depreciation, and important changes announced in the 1972 Budget included the introduction of a 100 per cent first-year allowance for all capital expenditure on plant and machinery throughout the United Kingdom. These capital allowances, together with the relief allowed since 1975 against stock appreciation, account for the declining trend in the effective rate of company taxation which can be observed in Table 4.3.

Selective employment tax
Selective employment tax was in operation for eight years from 1965 to 1973; it was designed to serve a number of purposes, including the raising of additional revenue and the broadening of the base of indirect taxation to include services. In addition, it sought to provide assistance to the manufacturing sector, both to strengthen exports and to generate economic growth, while also encouraging increased efficiency in services by raising relative labour costs. To achieve these objectives the tax was imposed on the employment of labour, refunds being provided to manufacturing industries. Initially, a slight subsidy was also given to employment in manufacturing through excess refunds and, although this subsidy was soon discontinued, provision for paying excess refunds to Development Areas was retained in the form of the Regional Employment Premium. Selective employment tax met with considerable criticism from the outset not only for technical reasons but on basic economic grounds. The tax was not a particularly satisfactory method of taxing services and, given the low rates at which it was levied, the size of any resulting shift of labour to manufacturing was questioned. More fundamentally, it seems extremely dubious in retrospect whether the choice of tax base was appropriate: the continuing poor performance of British manufacturing does not suggest that labour shortage was the main impediment to improved growth and export performance.

Value-added tax
In April 1973, purchase tax, selective employment tax and part of the

customs and excise duties on tobacco and alcoholic drinks were replaced by VAT. The new tax was intended to create 'a more broadly-based structure which, by discriminating less between different types of goods and services, would reduce the distortion of consumer choice'.[1] The establishment of VAT was central to EEC policy. The principal feature of the new tax was that for the first time in the United Kingdom it extended sales taxation to a wide range of service sectors, most notably the retail trade, but, to prevent the changeover having a regressive impact, large areas of essential expenditure which have by tradition been free of any direct imposition of tax (particularly food, fuel and power, public transport and housing) were relieved of VAT through exemption or zero rating. Despite a broadening of the base of the tax in the 1974 Budget, its effective coverage remains less than 60 per cent of consumers' expenditure, as compared with the 80-90 per cent envisaged by the EEC's proposed common system. The single rate of VAT was also quickly abandoned (in July 1974); a higher rate being introduced initially on petrol only, but from May 1975 on a wide range of 'luxury' goods.

Personal income and capital taxation

Before the fiscal year 1973-4 an individual could be liable both to income tax at a standard rate and (if his income exceeded a certain amount) to surtax levied at differential rates which increased progressively with the amount of taxable income. In 1973 this dual system was replaced by a single unified tax, under which a broad band of income became taxable at a basic rate, with successive slices above this level being chargeable at graduated higher rates. At the same time, as has already been mentioned, the overlap between the personal income tax system and corporation tax, which from 1966 meant that dividends were subject to double taxation, was eliminated; the corporation tax charged on company distributions now counts as income tax so far as the recipient is concerned.

Further ideas for reform, which have as yet not come to fruition and are attended by some controversy, concern the unification of the tax and social security systems, which have not always worked in harmony, and the replacement of the personal income tax by an expenditure tax. In October 1972 the Conservative government issued a Green Paper proposing a form of negative income tax as a means of unifying the systems of personal income tax and of income maintenance.[2] This particular approach to the problem was not, however, accepted by the

---

[1] Treasury, *Value-added Tax*, Cmnd 4621, London, HMSO, 1971.
[2] Treasury, *Proposals for a Tax-credit System*, Cmnd 5116, London, HMSO, 1972.

following Labour administration, and as yet proposals for harmonising the two systems command little consensus. The Report of the Meade Committee discusses the alternatives available;[1] it also revives another idea for reform — the replacement of income tax by a direct form of expenditure tax, where all of a person's savings (and investments) would be exempt from tax and only the residual amount of his income would be taxed as expenditure. Though attractive as a method of taxation, such a reform is baulked by considerable transitional difficulties.

One advantage of a direct expenditure tax is that it would make a separate capital gains tax unnecessary, since these would automatically be covered by an expenditure tax if they were spent. Capital gains taxation is a relatively new addition to the tax system. Only in 1962 did speculative capital gains on a wide range of property and asset holdings become liable to income tax. This was followed, in 1965, by a capital gains tax applicable to longer-term gains, the distinction between short-term and long-term gains being finally removed in the 1971 Budget.

Taxes on transfers of property on death have a much longer history. Estate duty, which related the amount of tax to the circumstances of the donor, dated from the end of the nineteenth century. It was eventually reformed in 1975 into a capital transfer tax,[2] which extended the taxation of transfers of wealth to cover gifts as well as legacies. Attempts to introduce a more comprehensive wealth tax have been unsuccessful because of the extreme difficulties involved in making it fair and administratively feasible. In 1974 the Treasury introduced a Green Paper outlining a scheme for a comprehensive annual wealth tax,[3] but a Parliamentary Select Committee failed to agree on the scheme and published a number of minority reports. The idea of a wealth tax is therefore, for the moment, in abeyance.

5. Nationalized Industries

A number of basic industries, fuel and power (other than petroleum), transport and communication, and iron and steel were taken into government ownership in the late 1940s. Steel was denationalized in 1954 and renationalized in 1965. The nationalization of these basic industries was a major political transformation, the result of forces which had been developing over many years.

Since nationalization each industry has had its own special problems. In some these were created by strongly increasing demand,

---

[1] Institute for Fiscal Studies, *The Structure and Reform of Direct Taxation*, London, Allen & Unwin, 1978.

[2] Treasury, *Capital Transfer Tax*, Cmnd 5705, London, HMSO, 1974.

[3] Treasury, *Wealth Tax*, Cmnd 5704, London, HMSO, 1974.

while in others, particularly coal and the railways, the problem was falling demand. But there were also common problems associated with the role of the industries in the economy and their relations with the government and Parliament.

The government's objectives were set out in the nationalization Statutes: first, the Boards which were set up to run the industries had a duty to raise revenues that, taking one year with another, would be not less than sufficient to meet all items properly chargeable to revenue; secondly, the industries were to be operated in the public interest. Boards were made responsible to Parliament for the overall financial position of the industries, while ministers were given powers to control investment and borrowing.

Dissatisfaction with the conduct of the industries in the 1950s, both inside and outside Parliament, led to the setting up of a Select Committee on the nationalized industries, which proceeded to a series of investigations into each undertaking. At about the same time the industries were required to borrow from the Treasury rather than on the market as had been the practice.

During the 1960s there were two White Papers on the financial and economic obligations of the nationalized industries, which attempted to set out new guidelines for their operation.[1] The 1961 White Paper emphasized that, although the industries had obligations of a national and non-commercial kind, they were not and ought not to be regarded as social services absolved from economic and social justification. It went on to note that some Boards were not making large enough provisions to cover the replacement cost of assets having regard to inflation and to provide against obsolescence. It noted the low returns obtained by some industries and pointed out that as a consequence the nationalized industries depended heavily on the savings of others to finance their investment. The White Paper explained how the Statutes should be interpreted with the aim of encouraging the Boards to increase revenue and prevent poor performance.

Following the publication of this White Paper specific financial objectives were set up for most of the industries for periods of up to five years, but the financial performance of the industries showed little improvement during the early 1960s. There was some increase in their gross trading surpluses in 1962 and 1963, but by 1964 the borrowing requirement was again rising rapidly.

The unsatisfactory position led to a further White Paper in 1967.

---

[1] Treasury, *The Financial and Economic Obligations of the Nationalized Industries*, Cmnd 1337, London, HMSO, 1961; *Nationalized Industries: a review of economic and financial objectives*, Cmnd 3437, London, HMSO, 1967.

This started from the position that the industries should be operated basically as commercial concerns and have the objectives of promoting an efficient allocation and use of resources. It laid down guiding principles for price policy and investment decisions; the technique of discounted cash flows was to be used for all important projects in the investment programmes. In addition to recovering accounting costs, prices were to be reasonably related to long-run marginal costs. Critical attention was to be paid to reducing costs and there was to be a continuous drive to increase efficiency and productivity. The system of financial targets would continue but should be interpreted more flexibly. All major price increases should be referred to the National Board for Prices and Incomes, which was also given powers to inquire into the efficiency of the industries when proposals for price increases were referred to it.

In the years following the 1967 White Paper the investment criteria came increasingly to be adopted as a useful discipline. But there were major difficulties in applying marginal-cost pricing. There was, however, a trend towards the application of more complex tariffs designed to reflect the costs of peak demand, so that time-differentiated tariffs are now used for electricity, telephones, railways and airlines, although differential charging is not carried to the optimal solution in marginal cost pricing. In the coal industry and on the railways the application of the new criteria was especially difficult. In the coal industry the main problem was that of ensuring the progression to a smaller efficient industry and the elimination of some pits which were losing heavily. The declining demand for railway transport meant that the railways Board could not eliminate its deficit by raising charges; the best it found it could do was to try to keep charges in line with general inflation. Where new investment was involved, it was, as a rule, only undertaken when the demand permitted charges which would cover costs.

The financial performance of the industries improved somewhat during the late 1960s, but conflicts with national economic policy led to a deterioration at the end of the decade. Prices and incomes policies were intensified and the industries were forced to delay price increases in line with price restraint. In mid-1974 the government attempted to reduce the nationalized industries' losses by permitting some large increases in the prices of electricity and coal, and in railway fares and telephone charges. The financial deficit of the industries reached nearly £3,000 million in 1975. However, it fell back in 1976 and 1977 as the gross trading surpluses increased and more than offset the rise in gross capital formation.

There were also broad government objectives relating to transport policy and fuel policy which sometimes conflicted with the main financial objectives. For example, it was argued that prudence dictated the maintenance of the coal industry in view of the uncertainty about supplies and costs of imported fuels. Similarly, a consideration of future transport needs implied that an efficient railway system would be needed, even though commercial operation in the 1960s would not have sustained the railways as a going concern. An uncontrolled run-down of the coal industry and the closure of some railway lines would also have conflicted with the government's regional policy.

Chapter 5

FINANCIAL INSTITUTIONS AND MONETARY POLICY

The first part of this chapter reviews the various kinds of financial institution in the United Kingdom. It is appropriate to start with the Bank of England as the central bank. Banks in the private sector, which are of special interest to the economist because their deposits are a major part of the money supply, merit separate treatment. Financial institutions which fall outside the official definition of the banking system are then described. The final section of this part deals with the standing regulations imposed on the financial insitutions by the Bank of England. The second part of the chapter describes the operation of discretionary monetary policy; the first section deals with policy objectives and the second with the instruments used to try to achieve those objectives.

1. Financial Institutions

Bank of England
Although the Bank of England only became publicly owned in 1946, its role as the monetary 'authority' had long been established. It no longer does much ordinary banking business, offering such services only to a vestige of private customers. Its important function is as central bank of the United Kingdom.

A distinction is drawn between the Issue Department — responsible for regulating the issue of bank notes — and the Banking Department — holding the principal bank account of the government (through which claims against the government are settled) and handling the sale of government stock and Treasury bills to the private sector. The Bank underpins the stability of the financial system in its capacity as 'lender of last resort'. In the field of monetary policy, as well as advising the government, it exercises control by dealing in the market for public debt, by manipulating its discount rate (formerly Bank Rate, now minimum lending rate) and by issuing requests or instructions to financial institutions; it also manages the country's foreign exchange business. In conjunction with the Treasury it is responsible for foreign exchange control, which regulates foreign exchange transactions. The Exchange Equalization Account, which holds the official reserves, is managed by the Bank, which itself deals in the foreign exchange market at times in order to influence the exchange rate.

Banks

The private banking sector includes four main groups: clearing banks, discount houses, the National Giro and the remainder — accepting houses, overseas and other banks.

The first of these groups is dominated by four London clearing banks — Barclays, Lloyds, the Midland and the National Westminster — which have thousands of branches throughout the country and a very large number of individual customers. The clearing banks may be distinguished from other financial institutions in that they play a major role in operating the country's system of payments; the transfer of a bank deposit from one person to another by the exchange of a cheque is a very common method of settling a debt. As well as current accounts, which companies and individuals hold in order to withdraw cash on demand, issue cheques and make use of various other money transmission services, the clearing banks take interest-bearing deposits. Seven-day deposits, which are mainly small savings from the personal sector, are technically subject to seven days' notice of withdrawal (although this requirement is often waived in practice) and carry only a relatively low rate of interest. Wholesale deposits of large sums (over £10,000) by companies and financial institutions and fixed-interest fixed-term securities, known as certificates of deposit, earn higher rates of interest.

Until the late 1960s nearly all clearing bank deposits were current accounts or seven-day deposits; official controls prevented the banks from attracting wholesale deposits. Deposit rates were linked by agreement to Bank Rate and the clearing banks were unable to issue certificates of deposit in their own names. Following the dismantling of the controls by the reforms of 1971,[1] wholesale deposits grew very rapidly, reaching 45 per cent of the sterling deposits of the London clearing banks by 1973.

Deposits, which are the liabilities of the banking sector to the public, are matched by lending to the other sectors of the economy. The banking sector's balance sheet (Table 5.1) reveals that banks channel deposits from the personal sector and non-residents to the company sector and the government. Bank finance is used by industry for fixed investment and working capital. Borrowing from banks is also the residual source of finance for the public sector; any excess of public expenditure over revenue (including receipts from sales of debt to the public) is held in the form of bank deposits which the banks use to buy government stock or Treasury bills.

Discount houses are concerned exclusively with buying and selling

[1] 'Competition and credit control', *Bank of England Quarterly Bulletin*, vol. 11, June 1971.

Table 5.1. *United Kingdom banking sector: domestic liabilities and assets outstanding at end-1977*

	Sources of funds		Lending	
	(£bn)	(%)	(£bn)	(%)
Public sector	1.5	3.6	17.3	30.5
Company sector	19.2	45.7	30.4	53.6
Personal sector	21.3	50.7	9.0	15.9
Total	42.0[a]	100.0	56.7[a]	100.0

SOURCE: CSO, *Financial Statistics.*
[a]Difference accounted for by overseas liabilities (net) of £7 billion *plus* non-deposit liabilities (net) of £7.7 billion.

assets in the money market. Their main source of funds is very short loans ('call and overnight money') from within the banking sector. At the end of 1977, 90 per cent of their borrowed funds was raised in this way. Historically the discount houses traded in commercial bills of exchange. They now operate also in a wider range of short-term assets − most important are Treasury bills, but also certificates of deposit, local authority bills and short-term government bonds. There are close relations between the discount houses and the Bank of England which play an important role in the management of the money market. There is an understanding that the houses will underwrite each week's tender issue of Treasury bills − a funding operation that covers short-term imbalances between the government's spending and receipts. In its capacity as lender of last resort the Bank stands ready to lend to the discount market when it is short of cash. Such loans are usually for one week at minimum lending rate, although they can be at higher rates for shorter periods. It is through the discount market that the Bank of England seeks to influence short-term interest rates − either by manipulating the balance of demand and supply of Treasury bills, or by direct instruction to the houses to alter their bid price.

The residual group of accepting houses, overseas and other banks undertakes a varied range of banking business, but tends to deal mainly with large sums of money and rarely offers money transmission services. As with the discount houses, the traditional role of accepting houses was as acceptors of bills of exchange. They now have other, quite different, functions, including floating share issues for companies wishing to raise capital and acting as trustees and investment advisers to bodies such as pension funds, trade unions and charities with large sums to invest. London branches of American, European and other foreign banks operate extensively in the Euro-currency markets, accepting interest-bearing deposits denominated in a foreign currency and then re-lending these funds either in the same currency or in sterling. In the last two decades this sector has grown very rapidly, much faster than the rest of the banking system. This growth has been associated with the development since the early 1960s of 'parallel' money markets, most notably the Euro-dollar market and the market for local authority finance. The activities of the clearing banks and discount houses in the new markets were restricted before 1971 by government policy or their own conventions.

The National Giro was inaugurated in 1968, it operates through the Post Office and is designed to facilitate money transfers. Although it is not usually thought of as a bank, it is defined for statistical purposes as part of the banking system. It offers cheap credit account facilities without any of the other services provided by the clearing banks and tends mainly to attract individuals or small firms with a large number of payments or receipts. Its gross deposits at the end of 1977 amounted to less than ¼ per cent of those of the banking system as a whole.

Other financial institutions

There are over 400 building societies, ranging in size from the large national societies to one-branch institutions. They are non-profitmaking and their depositors are their shareholders. Their funds are mainly the investments of small savers and take the form of shares and ordinary deposits. Deposits carry a slightly lower rate of interest than shares, but rank ahead of them in the event of a liquidation; however, as there is in practice virtually no danger of a society failing, only a small proportion of the societies' total funds are received as deposits. By the end of 1977 their total shares and deposits amounted to £32 billion, which is greater than the sterling deposits of the London clearing banks, although as late as 1963 their resources were barely half those of the clearing banks. On the other side of the balance sheet, the principal assets of building societies are mortgage loans for house purchase. In this country clearing banks do not normally offer mortgages and the societies dominate the mortgage market. In 1977 over 45 per cent of new loans to the personal sector for house purchase were building society mortgages.

Finance houses provide instalment credit, usually in the form of hire purchase, but increasingly in the form of personal loans, to individuals and companies wishing to buy consumer durables, or plant and machinery. Their main sources of funds are deposits from the secondary banks and overdrafts from the clearing banks, although some of the larger houses have branches which accept deposits from individuals.

Insurance companies and pension funds mainly use the funds they receive as premiums and pension contributions to buy long-term assets — company securities, government bonds and property; they are also important buyers of new share business. As the size of their funds, particularly pension funds, has grown, their position and power in the stock market have become increasingly important.

There are also two principal types of collective investment institutions — investment trusts and unit trusts — whose assets are shares in other companies, usually public and quoted on the Stock Exchange. Shares in investment trusts are themselves traded on the Stock Exchange, whereas 'units' in a unit trust, which can be compared with the American mutual fund, are bought and sold at a price calculated to reflect the value of the assets, and declared by the managers, usually daily. Over the past decade there has been a rapid growth in the market share of unit trusts, but they still represent a very small proportion of the whole market in equities.

Special investment agencies have been established since 1945 to provide medium-term and long-term capital to companies which have difficulty raising it from other sources. The most important are the Finance Corporation for Industry and the Industrial and Commercial Finance Corporation. The former lends sums of over £2 million for the re-equipment and development of industry. The latter offers financial advice and computer and other services, as well as loans, to small and medium-sized companies. Generally its loans are less than £2 million for seven to twenty years at fixed interest rates. In 1974 these two institutions were grouped under a single holding company known as Finance for Industry. Its initial share capital was held by the London and Scottish clearing banks and the Bank of England, but when it was expanded in November 1974 other financial institutions also agreed to subscribe.

The London and provincial Stock Exchange trading floors in the United Kingdom and the Irish Republic are now grouped into a single dealing system for quoted securities, both public sector and private. Business is introduced by brokers who work on commission for buyers and sellers. Brokers must deal through jobbers, who make a market in stocks, which they deal in on their own account. New capital for industry and commerce can be raised through the Stock Exchange by share issues. Nearly all securities issued on the British market are in registered form. United Kingdom residents who hold bearer securities are required to deposit them with an authorised depository — a stockbroker, a bank or some other professional intermediary.

The government also competes directly in the small savers' market. Facilities include National Savings certificates and British Savings Bonds (both securities with maturity dates), Save As You Earn (a contractual savings scheme), Premium Savings Bonds (on which accumulated interest is distributed as prizes determined by lot) and facilities offering small savers easy access to government stocks. The National and Trustee Savings Banks accept deposits and offer interest-bearing, on-call and long-term accounts. The Trustee Savings Banks, which also run current accounts, are expected to expand their range of services in due course. Many of the national savings facilities attract tax reliefs.

Flows of funds of the personal sector and industry
Table 5.2, which shows the financial transactions of the personal sector and non-financial companies during the period 1973-7, gives an idea of the relative importance of the various financial institutions as borrowers from, and lenders to, the personal sector and industry. Financial intermediaries transfer funds from sectors with a current surplus to those with a current deficit. Thus, insurance companies channel savings from the personal sector, which is usually in surplus, to the company and public sectors, which are usually in deficit, by employing life assurance and pension funds to buy company securities and government bonds. Similarly, the banking system acts as a medium through which personal sector deposits help to finance the borrowing of industry and the government.

Table 5.2 *Transactions in financial assets, annual averages 1973-7*

£ billions

	Personal sector	Non-financial companies
Assets (saving)		
Cash	0.4	0.4
Bank deposits	1.8	1.3
Building society deposits	3.5	0.2
UK company securities	−1.5	—
Public sector debt	1.9	0.2
Life insurance policies	4.8	—
Total	*10.9*	*2.1*
Liabilities (borrowing)		
Bank loans	0.6	3.0
Building society loans	2.7	—
Hire purchase credit	0.1	—
Share capital	—	0.6
Total	*3.4*	*3.6*
Other transactions[a]	−1.0	−0.2
Net acquisition of financial assets	6.5	−1.7

SOURCE: CSO, *Financial Statistics.*
[a]Includes statistical discrepancy.

Monetary and credit controls
The new regulations for financial institutions were drawn up in 1971

and reflect changes which had taken place during the 1960s, particularly the growth of the secondary banks. Their aim is to allow the authorities some control over the activities of the institutions without unduly interfering with competition between them or discriminating between different types of institution.

The regulations and directives imposed by the Bank of England are observed voluntarily, but powers exist under the Bank of England Act 1946 to give them the force of law if necessary. They fall into two groups: standing day-to-day rules and those which the Bank invokes from time to time as circumstances warrant.

The standing regulations require that all banks hold 12½ per cent of certain liabilities (chiefly sterling deposits of less than two years maturity, net foreign currency liabilities, net inter-bank sterling deposits and net sterling certificates of deposit) in certain assets. These are largely 'traditional' money market assets: balances at the Bank of England, Treasury bills, money at call with the London discount market, government stocks with a maturity of one year or less, local authority and commercial bills eligible for re-discount at the Bank of England and company tax reserve certificates. The banks themselves can determine what proportion of each asset they hold, except for commercial bills, which must not contribute more than 2 per cent, and the deposit banks' holdings of cash at the Bank of England, which must contribute at least 1½ per cent. The supply of these assets is largely under the control of the authorities, so that they can make it easier or more difficult for the banks to make up their minimum reserve ratios. However, eligible liabilities include *net* inter-bank deposits and issues of sterling certificates of deposit, which means that a bank can reduce its liabilities and thus increase its reserve ratio by lending to other banks and bidding for sterling certificates of deposit. There are special arrangements for the Northern Ireland banks in view of their particular relations with the Republic of Ireland and the financial needs arising out of the present emergency.

Finance houses must hold 10 per cent of their eligible liabilities (all deposits for less than two years other than those from banks) in the same assets.

The arrangements for discount houses were changed in July 1973, so that their total assets, excluding certain ones from the public sector (largely of less than five years to maturity), must not exceed twenty times their capital and reserves. Although there is no longer any formal requirement to hold public sector debt, the Bank of England will only act as lender of last resort against approved securities, particularly Treasury bills.

2. Monetary Policy

Objectives

Monetary policy is determined by the Treasury in consultation with the Bank of England and is administered by the Bank. Its objectives are the same as those of macroeconomic policy generally, namely price stability, economic growth, full employment and balance of payments equilibrium.

For most of the postwar period domestic monetary policy aimed to influence demand by regulating the availability of credit from financial institutions and manipulating short-term interest rates. In general, monetary policy was considered subordinate to fiscal policy in demand management and there was no target for the growth of the money supply on either of the official definitions, although policy was to some extent influenced by the idea that the money supply should accomodate the real growth of the economy plus an 'acceptable' rate of inflation.

In recent years monetary policy has been given much greater emphasis. Since 1976 targets have been announced for domestic credit expansion (DCE), which may be loosely defined as the change in the money supply adjusted for the direct effect of balance of payments surplus or deficit, and the growth of the broadly defined money stock M3 (that is, notes and coin in circulation, together with all bank deposits denominated in sterling and all deposits held by United Kingdom residents in other currencies). There were a number of reasons for this reappraisal of the conventional methods of monetary policy. During the early 1970s the economic doctrine known as 'monetarism' came increasingly to have a bearing on policy objectives and policy formulation, a process which was assisted by the intervention of the IMF during the 1967 and 1976 balance of payments crises. The high rate of inflation in recent years has made it very difficult for the authorities to frame monetary policy in terms of nominal interest rates and the introduction of monetary targets was also seen as a way of helping to restore confidence to financial markets which had been unsettled by events following the changes inaugurated in 1971.

Before 1972, while exchange parities were fixed, external pressures arising from a weakening balance of payments appeared to be the main influence on monetary policy. The Bank of England was obliged to raise short-term interest rates or deal in the foreign exchange market to prevent the exchange rate moving outside prescribed limits. Since December 1971 interventions in the foreign exchange market have been largely confined to attempts to counter erratic fluctuations in the rate caused by short-term capital flows, although the United Kingdom's international price competitiveness has also been a matter of concern.

Instruments

Ever since the late nineteenth century the Bank of England has sought to manage the level of short-term interest rates. Before 1972 the key short-term rate, Bank Rate — which is what the Bank charged on loans to the discount houses — was fixed administratively. Other short-term rates, such as banks' deposit and lending rates, were allowed only very limited variation relative to Bank Rate. In October 1972 Bank Rate was superseded by minimum lending rate, which was linked to the Treasury bill rate, normally being ½ per cent higher rounded to the nearest ¼ per cent. This formula was overriden in exceptional circumstances, such as during the oil crisis in November 1973, when the minimum lending rate was raised from 11¼ per cent to 13 per cent. In May 1978 the formula was abandoned entirely and the rate is now determined by administrative decision, any changes normally being announced at 12.30 p.m. on a Thursday. This does not, however, mean a complete reversion to the rigidities of the old Bank Rate, which was changed only very rarely; it is intended that the rate should be readily adjustable and depend on market developments.

Since 1971 the authorities have usually sought to manipulate the level of short-term interest rates through the market in Treasury bills. Every week there is an issue of three-month Treasury bills, the size of which is determined by short-term financing and general policy needs. They are bought largely by the banks themselves and on their behalf by the discount houses, as they are an important component of the banks' minimum reserve ratios. The Bank of England can influence a range of interest rates by varying the size and thus the price of the Treasury bill issue. If the discount houses are unable to cover the issue, they have the right to borrow cash from the Bank of England, usually for one week at the minimum lending rate, although this can vary. As this is a penal rate, the discount houses must increase the rates they charge the banks in order to maintain their margins.

The lending policies of banks have been subjected to discretionary controls of various kinds. Quantitative ceilings were imposed from time to time between 1955 and 1971. Such restrictions on lending by the clearing banks, which contributed to the expansion of the secondary banking sector, were officially abandoned in 1971. Qualitative requests, the usual objective of which has been to channel lending to priority sectors, were also used during the 1950s and 1960s and, unlike quantitative ceilings, are extant. Banks are normally requested to look with favour on applications for loans to finance exports and productive investment, but with disfavour on applications for loans by the personal sector and property companies. Calls for Special Deposits have been made from time to time since July 1958; when this happens, each bank is required to lodge a certain proportion of its eligible deposits with the Bank of England. It is, however, possible for banks to make the necessary portfolio adjustment by running down their investments in government bonds, thus avoiding any reduction in advances. Calls for Special Deposits have at times been accompanied by a request for the adjustment in assets to be made by reducing advances rather than investments but, by definition, the call is not then a substitute for direct instruction to the banks. The supplementary Special Deposits scheme (popularly called 'the corset') was first introduced in November 1973. This scheme operates by requiring banks to lodge with the Bank of England non-interest-bearing Special Deposits if their interest-bearing eligible deposits exceed a specified ceiling. Once the ceiling has been reached the scheme makes it unprofitable for banks to finance an expansion in lending by bidding for wholesale deposits.

The availability of credit from finance houses has not been regulated by requests or calls for Special Deposits, but rather by variations in the statutory regulations prescribing the terms − the minimum size of the deposit required and the maximum length of the repayment time − according to which hire purchase transactions may be made. During the 1950s and 1960s changes in consumer credit terms, which unlike most other monetary measures were considered to have quick-acting and predictable effects upon consumers' expenditure, were an important policy instrument. However, the effect of hire purchase restrictions falls on a very narrow component of total spending, chiefly on durable goods. The Crowther Report recommended that, mainly because of the distortions to the credit markets that resulted from the use of such discriminatory controls, they should be removed.[1] With the lifting of restrictions in July 1971 it was widely assumed that the authorities had renounced their use as an economic regulator. However, in the event, there was reluctance to abandon this policy weapon and new restrictions were imposed in December 1973.

Although there has been no formal control over mortgage advances, the authorities have at times sought to influence building society lending and interest rates. This has usually been done informally by 'persuasion', although an official loan was made to the societies in 1974, when they were acutely short of funds, to prevent them raising interest rates or rationing advances.

---

[1] Department of Trade and Industry, *Consumer Credit. Report of the Committee*, Cmnd 4596, London, HMSO, 1971.

Chapter 6

EXTERNAL TRADE AND PAYMENTS

1. General Structure of the Balance of Payments

The United Kingdom has had a deficit on visible trade in all but a few years since the beginning of the nineteenth century. Usually the deficit has been more than matched by a surplus on invisible transactions, but between the First and Second World Wars this was tending to dwindle, while at the same time exports were declining in both value and volume, although imports were rather more stable. Consequently the balance of payments on current account is believed to have been in slight deficit in the years immediately preceding the Second World War.

In the postwar period the deficit on visible trade increased sharply (Table 6.1); it reached a peak of £5,235 million in 1974. The growing deficit partly reflected the rise in turnover. In 1974 the visible deficit was about a quarter of the value of imports of goods; in 1937 it had been more than a third. In real terms, the comparison is even more favourable, imports having risen less than threefold and exports more than fourfold. For manufactures, on the other hand, the story is rather different, partly no doubt because of the dominating position of

Table 6.1 *United Kingdom balance of payments, 1920-77*

£ *millions*

	Visible trade (net)	Invisibles (net)	Current balance	Capital flows (net)	Balancing item	Official financing
1920	−148	+463	+315	−135	−132	−48
1929	−263	+339	+76	−111	+27	+8
1937	−336	+279	−57	+85	+101	−129
1950	−51	+358	+307	+128	+140	−575
1955	−313	+158	−155	−195	+121	+229
1963	−89	+218	+129	−99	−88	+58
1967	−567	+273	−294	−497	+225	+566
1971	+261	+829	+1,090	+1,809	+247	−3,146
1977	−1,709	+1,998	+289	+4,410	+2,662	−7,361

SOURCES: CSO, *United Kingdom Balance of Payments 1972* and *United Kingdom Balance of Payments 1967-1977*, London, HMSO, 1972 and 1978; *Bank of England Quarterly Bulletin*, March 1974.

United Kingdom products at the beginning of the period. Between 1937 and 1974 imports of manufactures increased in volume more than twice as much as total imports, while exports of manufactures increased at the same rate as the total.

There has been a sharp improvement since 1974, partly explained by the beginning of oil production in the North Sea. The value of this output in 1977 was over £2 billion, of which about a third was exported and two-thirds used to reduce oil imports. The deficit on trade in crude oil was still substantially bigger than it had been in 1973 before the rise in the oil price, but the other components of the visible balance also became more favourable between 1974 and 1977. The surplus on manufactures rose steeply, with export volume increasing slightly faster than import volume although trends have since worsened.

From 1925 until 1935 the United Kingdom's terms of trade improved, reaching a level that was only gradually regained through the 1950s and 1960s after a sharp deterioration in the late 1940s and early 1950s. The interwar improvement partly compensated for the worsening in the balance of trade in real terms, while the early postwar deterioration reduced the effect of the relative increase in the volume of exports. In 1973, however, because of the rise in commodity prices, the terms of trade moved violently against the United Kingdom and they have since stabilized at a level not much more favourable than that prevailing at the time of the Korean War.

The problem of a visible deficit has not in the past been as serious for the United Kingdom as for other developed countries, although if present trends continue it will become increasingly important. The United Kingdom was able to tolerate rapid growth in the volume of imports in the 1930s and 1950s partly because of favourable terms of trade. But from the beginning of the 1960s until about 1973-5, when the rise in external prices followed by the growing importance of North Sea oil output made it inappropriate, the intention was broadly that a surplus on invisible account should finance a small trade deficit, an outflow of capital (first principally as investment, recently as aid) and any desired increase in the reserves. As the United Kingdom's widespread overseas commitments (including those to the EEC) imply a substantial and rising deficit on government account, this requires an even bigger surplus on private sector invisibles. The invisible balance has always in fact been positive, but from the middle of 1972 to 1976 the surplus was too small to offset the increased deficit on visible trade. Since 1970 the capital account, previously only in surplus in 1960, has been increasingly important as a source of finance for the visible deficit. The net flow of capital for private investment had previously been inward only in occasional years, but substantial net inflows were recorded from 1974 to 1977 because of increased oil company investment. The public sector capital account had its first large net inflow in 1973 and this has remained a major source of finance. Apart from these long-term capital inflows, which, in the private sector at least, may continue for some years, the other main source of finance until 1974 (as in the late 1940s) was the building up of sterling reserves by other countries.

It will probably not be possible to return to an aim of an invisible surplus. The surplus on property income may be turned into a deficit by the interest and profits accruing to foreign participants in the exploitation of the oil, and this and the increasing government payments to the EEC will offset the surplus on services. But the surplus on non-oil trade that was usual before 1973 had been restored by 1976 and the contribution of North Sea oil should bring the net cost of oil imports below the 1973 level by 1980. In the mid-1980s net exports of oil could temporarily reverse the traditional deficit on visible trade and thus make it possible to achieve the postwar goal of current surplus. Despite the exceptionally high level to which the reserves had risen by the end of 1977, such a surplus is still likely to be needed in the 1980s to repay official debt incurred to finance the deficits of the mid-1970s.

2. The Commonwealth Preference and Sterling Area Systems
Perhaps the outstanding feature of British commercial policy over the fifty years prior to membership of the EEC was the establishment and subsequent dissolution of preferential arrangements of various kinds in favour of the Commonwealth and Sterling Area.

Though membership of the two areas overlapped to an important extent, there were in fact two systems, differing both in coverage and in organization. The Commonwealth Preference Area comprised all members of the Commonwealth, South Africa and the Irish Republic; the Sterling Area excluded one major Commonwealth country — Canada — and included a number of other countries, varying from time to time, within the British sphere of influence either politically or commercially.

Though the United Kingdom gave and received some preferential tariff treatment in the 1920s, most goods then entered the country duty-free from all sources. The Commonwealth Preference system originated in 1932, when duties were introduced on virtually all manufactures and some foodstuffs. Under the Ottawa Agreements, Commonwealth foodstuffs were charged lower rates of duty than imports from the rest of the world; imports of manufactures from the Commonwealth, then a small fraction of British imports, were generally exempt from duty.

The introduction of exchange controls and dollar pooling for the

Sterling Area during the Second World War marked the beginning of a formally defined area. For its overseas members whose currencies were linked to the pound sterling, the change was from keeping reserves in London from habit and for convenience to being expected not only to keep them there but to accept co-ordination of their use according to the needs of the area as whole. Freedom of action was particularly limited for some of the colonial countries, where the domestic currency issue still required complete sterling backing, and the only complete exception to the general rule was the Union of South Africa, which continued to keep a high proportion of its reserves in gold. The pooling and restrictions represented a reversal of the trend of the 1930s towards a reduction in effective United Kingdom direction of the monetary policies of the Sterling Area countries, particularly the independent ones.

In the early years after the Second World War the existence of exchange controls on payments to and from non-Sterling Areas gave the Sterling Area a further stimulus because of its exemption from the United Kingdom's controls. The United Kingdom also gave uniform and preferential quota treatment to Sterling Area products, and it gave uniform tariff treatment to goods originating in the Commonwealth Preference Area.[1] This uniformity was not reciprocated, however. Many Commonwealth countries gave British goods no tariff preferences or very few; some Sterling Area countries operated a generalized system of quotas and exchange controls that gave no preference to imports from other Sterling Area countries.

In the 1930s the United Kingdom had provided other Commonwealth and Sterling Area countries, particularly the food producers, with a stable market; the central control of imports in the 1940s permitted long-term contracts that had a similar effect. In the 1950s and especially in the 1960s, however, trade liberalization and the growth of markets outside the Preference Area reduced the significance of preferential trading arrangements as they had previously existed and over the last fifteen or twenty years they have been drastically re-orientated: the system of Commonwealth Preference and the Sterling Area was first eroded and then, in the process of negotiating entry to the EEC, deliberately dismantled.

The restraints of the early postwar years, which had been directed at discouraging expenditure outside the Sterling Area, and particularly

---

[1] In one special case, sugar, the United Kingdom paid negotiated prices on fixed quantities of imports from the Commonwealth under the Commonwealth Sugar Agreement, the negotiated prices normally being well above world prices. In war and early postwar years it had operated a number of other commodity long-term bulk-purchasing agreements, but these had effectively disappeared by the early 1960s.

in Dollar Area countries, lapsed for the independent Sterling Area countries as early as the 1950s. Such preferences as Overseas Sterling Area countries had given to Britain and to one another by means of exchange controls and quotas virtually disappeared, as did the similar preferences accorded by the United Kingdom.

The Sterling Area remained in being after 1960 because exchange controls were not applied to investment by United Kingdom residents in the Overseas Sterling Area — a privilege abolished when the pound was floated in 1972 — but when sterling was devalued in November 1967 a number of Overseas Sterling Area countries did not change the par value of their own currencies correspondingly. These countries nevertheless continued to keep a large proportion of their foreign exchange reserves in British government assets. From 1968 onwards the United Kingdom guaranteed the greater part of these sterling reserves against devaluation by a series of agreements, in which Sterling Area countries undertook in return that the proportion of their reserves (though not the amount) held in sterling would be maintained at or above a prescribed figure. These arrangements were, however, allowed to lapse in 1974.

Meanwhile preferential margins in the United Kingdom tariff, which in 1961 was equivalent to about 7 per cent *ad valorem*, were being eroded in a number of ways. First, where duties were specific rather than *ad valorem*, rising prices steadily reduced the percentage preference margin. Secondly, where 'most favoured nation' duties on products paying no duty if imported from the Commonwealth into the United Kingdom — in practice most manufactured products — were reduced in the course of the GATT negotiations, the margin of preference was automatically reduced. Thirdly, the creation of the European Free Trade Association (EFTA) during the years 1959-67 diluted the effect of United Kingdom preferences to the Commonwealth by putting Commonwealth and EFTA manufactures on the same tariff footing. There is some evidence that this led to trade diversion in favour of EFTA. Finally, unilateral tariff changes led to the reduction or dilution of preferences, initially affecting only United Kingdom exports to the Commonwealth. However, at the beginning of 1972 the United Kingdom took two major steps: it introduced a preferential duty on Commonwealth cotton textiles and clothing, formerly duty-free, and a system of generalized preferences for manufactures other than textiles from developing countries, putting them on a par with the developing countries in the Commonwealth.

Thus, even had Britain not sought to join the EEC, the Commonwealth Preference and Sterling Area systems were rapidly declining in importance during the 1950s and 1960s; but this decision amounted to a death blow. The psychological impact of the abortive negotiations of 1957-8 was itself important, while the creation of EFTA, the free trade association of Britain, the Scandinavian countries, Portugal, Switzerland

and Austria, had a direct affect on trade between the United Kingdom and the Commonwealth. In the 1961-3 negotiations for entry into the EEC the United Kingdom was still seeking to retain some part of the Commonwealth Preference system, but by the time of the final negotiations for entry this special treatment had been reduced to medium-term guarantees on United Kingdom imports of Commonwealth sugar and New Zealand butter and cheese, association with the Community for some minor Commonwealth countries and territories,[1] and easier Community tariff treatment for a handful of products of interest to Commonwealth producers.

The first steps towards the abolition of tariffs between Britain and the enlarged Community were taken in 1973. In February of that year import levies replaced protective duties on goods covered by the CAP and at the beginning of April the first cut was made in rates of duty on industrial products imported from the rest of the Community. At the beginning of 1974 the first moves were made to assimilate to the Community's Common External Tariff duties charged by the United Kingdom on imports from non-Community countries (other than members of EFTA, with which duty-free trade continued). This entailed the introduction of duties on goods previously admitted free from the Commonwealth Preference Area. Over the next few years similar moves were made according to the timetable laid down in the Treaty of Accession, culminating on 1 July 1977 in the disappearance of customs duties on imports from the enlarged Community and the replacement of the British tariff by the Common External Tariff.

3. Trade Liberalization

The other major development of the postwar period in the sphere of trade policy has been the liberalization of trade on a multilateral basis, in common with all other industrial countries, through tariff reductions, and through the abolition of quantitative import restrictions and exchange controls.

As founder-member of the IMF and the Organization for European Economic Cooperation (OEEC), Britain directed its commercial policies during the 1950s towards restoring the convertibility of sterling (associated with the removal of exchange controls on current though not on capital transactions) and towards the abolition of quota restrictions on imports. Formal convertibility under article 8 of the IMF was adopted in 1961, but the pound had in effect been convertible for non-residents since February 1955, when the Exchange Equalization

---

[1] The major African Commonwealth countries already have association agreements with the Six, while Asian and developed Commonwealth countries are being treated like the rest of the world. In 1975 the EEC introduced preferential tariffs and increased quotas for some imports from developing countries.

Account began to support the rate for non-convertible sterling, previously sold for foreign exchange only at a discount.

Meanwhile, quota restrictions on Sterling Area imports, which had been of little significance since 1955, were effectively abolished in 1958. The removal of quotas on imports from the OEEC and the Dollar Area took slightly longer, until mid-1960 and 1961 respectively. Quotas on Japanese goods and imports from the Sino-Soviet bloc were maintained into the 1960s, but there was steady progress towards liberalization. In contrast, a system of quotas on imports of cotton textiles and clothing from developing countries was gradually built up over the same years. However, apart from this, some restrictions on imports from Sino-Soviet countries and a few quotas remaining on minor items, physical controls on United Kingdom imports had disappeared by the end of the 1960s.

Thus the sole major instrument of commercial policy, save in respect of farm produce, was then as it is now the tariff. Britain's 'most favoured nation' tariff always had negligible or zero duties on raw materials, but used to give considerable protection to manufactures in the 1930s. Tariff reductions from the early postwar tariff-cutting programme under GATT, which culminated in the Geneva Round of 1956, made little difference to this situation. As elsewhere, significant tariff reductions began with the Dillon Round and were carried on in the Kennedy Round on a greatly increased scale. Between 1960 and 1972 the United Kingdom's 'most favoured nation' tariff on manufactures was reduced by roughly two-fifths, with reductions of a half applying to a high proportion of finished goods, especially machinery and vehicles. At the beginning of 1972 the average United Kingdom tariff on non-agricultural goods was only a few percentage points higher than the Common External Tariff of the EEC, where formerly it had been considerably higher.

4. Exchange Rate Policy

Before the First World War sterling had been on the Gold Standard, but during and in the years immediately following the war convertibility into gold was suspended and the rate of exchange against the dollar fell. Notwithstanding the misgivings of J. M. Keynes, the great majority of financial leaders took the view that the fall was the result of temporary strain because of high imports and restricted exports and that convertibility should be restored, and at the pre-war rate. The decision to return to the prewar gold parity was thus treated as a timing decision rather than a decision about the appropriate rate. The rise in the rate in early 1925 was both a confirmation of this assumption and an indication that the timing could be brought forward. That adjustments to domestic prices might be needed was recognized, but this was treated as a necessary cost, not as a possible influence on the decision. The appreciation, followed by the failure of United States prices to rise as rapidly as expected and France's return to gold with a devaluation, made British exports uncompetitive in those markets in the late 1920s. The adjustments necessary to hold the restored parity proved to be impossible and, combined with the loss of confidence in other currencies, to threaten a flight of capital from sterling in 1931. The gold standard was accordingly abandoned for the rest of the 1930s.

The government did not intervene to slow the resulting fall in the value of the pound. But in 1932 when it began to recover (at about $3.50), control was introduced, directed at preventing disturbances in external markets from hurting domestic policy. The Exchange Equalization Account provided, through dealings in Treasury bills, some insulation from short-term capital flows. The value of the pound in terms of other currencies rose through the 1930s.

In 1944 a new international monetary system was agreed at Bretton Woods to establish parities for all member countries. The initial sterling rate was $4.03. An attempt to restore convertibility in 1947 under the terms of the 1945 Anglo-American loan agreement failed, and in September 1949 the rate was lowered to $2.80. For the United Kingdom this change was perhaps a reaction more to capital account problems than to import increases; controls still kept these to a low level. As the devaluation immediately preceded a large rise in commodity prices, it increased their effect. For the United Kingdom its size was, however, reduced by the number of countries inside and outside the Sterling Area that maintained their currencies' existing parities with the pound. The principal effect was thus to reinforce the planned diversion of imports from and exports to the Dollar Area by the Sterling Area as a whole.

Throughout the 1950s and the first half of the 1960s maintaining the parity unchanged was a central consideration in the United Kingdom's external policy. The ability to maintain the rate was helped by the introduction of swap arrangements among central banks. The possibility of devaluation to improve the current balance was discussed from the early 1960s, but, as in the 1920s, attempts were made to adjust the economy to the exchange rate, until huge short-term outflows made inevitable the movement to a lower rate $2.40) in November 1967. The subsequent improvement in the current balance was slow to materialize and was partly the result of growing world trade, but it was widely accepted as a demonstration of the success of the devaluation, and opposition to a more flexible exchange rate was correspondingly weakened. In 1971 the floating and devaluation of the dollar caused the pound to float for four months and, although the mistake of returning to an overvalued parity was made yet again, in the summer of

1972 floating and devaluation were no longer feared and unfamiliar and could be introduced without delay. From the end of 1972 to the end of 1976 the pound fell by a third (measured by the 'effective rate', its value in terms of a weighted average of other currencies), but early in 1977 it recovered slightly and up to the end of 1978 it had not changed significantly again (apart from a temporary rise at the end of 1977). The fall had occurred in discrete changes between temporary plateaux rather than continously, but this was the longest period of stability since floating began.

Measured by relative export prices or unit costs, there appears to have been little change in the United Kingdom's competitive position over the period 1972-7, as the fall in the exchange rate has roughly balanced higher British inflation. In the early period of floating, and under the conditions attached to the IMF financing in 1975-6, 'maintaining competitiveness' appears indeed to have been the government's policy. Subsequently, however, there seems to have been a return to a policy of maintaining a constant effective rate, which entailed resistance to upward pressure in 1977.

Movements in the exchange rate have of course affected the invisible balance and the capital account as well as visible trade. Property income, in particular, has risen through devaluation, as sterling-denominated payments abroad do not change, while foreign currency receipts increase in sterling terms. Such benefits will be reduced as payments denominated in foreign currency on loans from abroad become more important, but these would have to rise more than is probable before the situation would be completely reversed. Similarly, on capital account, the borrowing in non-sterling currency is a potential burden. But until the offering of exchange rate guarantees, which have now been withdrawn, devaluation, by increasing the sterling value of reserves of foreign currency, improved the ratio between these and short-term sterling liabilities.

5. Imports and Exports

The volume of imports of goods was about four times as great in 1976-7 as at the turn of the century (Table 6.2); it doubled in the first sixty years and subsequently it has more than doubled again. Two world wars, the great depression, and restrictions and import duties of varying severity hampered import development during the former period. On the other hand, from the early 1960s an unprecedented import growth accompanied the import liberalization measures already described and a rapid rise in home demand. In general, import growth lagged behind the increase in national product in volume terms during the first half of this century, but far outstripped it in later years, with imports of manufactures rising particularly fast. Until the beginning

Table 6.2 *Imports of goods, 1900-77*

Volume indices, 1961 = 100[a]

(A) Manufactures

	Finished manufactures			Chemicals	Textiles	Total
	Machinery	Transport equipment	Total			
1938	40	28	43	41	31	54
1950	29	23	25	44	65	43
1955	46	54	41	60	57	67
1956-63	78	106	81	88	22	86
1964-71	213	337	219	224	132	179
1972-5	476	847[b]	489[b]	406	230	331[b]
1976-7	553	1,114[b]	584[b]	482	271	336[b]

(B) All goods

	Manufactures	Food beverages, tobacco	Basic materials	Fuels	Total goods
1900					51
1913					68
1929					77
1938	54	98	96	29	76
1950	43	78	94	41	65
1955	67	89	102	75	82
1956-63	86	98	99	92	94
1964-71	179	103	106	172	138
1972-5	331	103	102	211	196[c]
1976-7	386[b]	103	100	163	211[c]

SOURCES: Department of Trade and Industry; London and Cambridge Economic Service, *Key Statistics of the British Economy 1900-1970*, London, Times, 1971; NIESR estimates.

[a]Indices based on 1954, 1961, 1970 and 1975 linked through overlapping years 1952-5, 1964-7 and 1975-7.

[b]From 1975 includes part of 'continental shelf' transactions.

[c]Includes gold coins; this inclusion is estimated to have added about 0.5 per cent to the volume index in 1974-5 and it would probably be less in previous years.

of the 1970s fuel imports also increased very rapidly, whereas imports of food, beverages and tobacco have throughout risen relatively slowly and the volume of basic materials imports was about the same in 1977 as forty years earlier.

In value terms the ratio of imports to national product changed little in the twenty-five years to 1972, import prices having risen much more slowly than domestic prices. There have, however, been big changes in the composition of imports. Imports of food, beverages and tobacco shrank from almost half of the total value in 1935-8 to about a sixth in 1976-7 and imports of basic materials accounted for only 10 per cent of all merchandise imports in 1976-7, compared with 26 per cent before the Second World War and about 30 per cent in the early 1950s (Table 6.3). On the other hand, fuel imports had, by the 1950s, grown from practically nothing at the turn of the century into a group which constituted about 10-12 per cent of the total for the next twenty years or so. In 1974 the share had risen to about 20 per cent as a result of the increase in oil prices, but in the late 1970s North Sea oil and gas began to reduce fuel imports. The share of the total accounted for by imports of manufactures rose in the 1970s to well over 50 per cent, although up to the mid-1950s it had been only about 20 per cent, as in 1935-8.

The volume of food imports rose by about 50 per cent between 1900 and 1937-8, but then remained below the 1937-8 level until the late 1950s. This was partly due to the incentives given to British agriculture during and after the war. But imports of food per head of the population during the last fifteen years have been on the whole lower than in the early 1960s. The volume of imports of basic materials has shown only relatively minor fluctuations over the last forty years, but imports per unit of manufacturing output fell by nearly three-fifths over the same period.

Falls in the ratio of imports of materials to industrial production were especially sharp during the two world wars, although apparently continuing on a much smaller scale in peacetime also.[1] The chief reasons have been the decline of the textile and other industries which are heavily dependent on imported materials, and partial replacement by synthetic products of natural fibres and rubber, and the new applications of manufactured materials as substitutes for natural ones, for example the use of steel instead of timber in building.

---

[1] M.FG. Scott, *A Study of United Kingdom Imports*, Cambridge University Press, 1963, pp. 28-9. On a definition which includes non-ferrous metals, Scott estimates that imports of materials increased by about 40 per cent from 1900 to 1938.

Table 6.3 *Changes in the composition of imports*[a] *1935-77*

Percentages

	1935-8[b]	1948-55	1956-63	1964-71	1972-5	1976-7
Machinery[c]	3	2	5	10	13	14
Transport equipment	1	1	2	4	7	8
Chemicals	2	3	4	6	6	7
Textiles and clothing	3	3	3	4	5	5
Other manufactures	12	11	14	22	23	23
Total manufactures	*21*	*20*	*28*	*46*	*54*	*57*
Food, beverages and tobacco	47	39	37	26	18	16
Basic materials	26	32	23	16	11	10
Fuels	5	9	12	11	16	16
Total non-manufactures	*78*	*80*	*72*	*53*	*45*	*42*
Total goods[d]	100	100	100	100	100	100

SOURCES: W. Beckerman and Associates, *The British Economy in 1975*, Cambridge University Press, 1965, p. 149, Table 5.1; Department of Trade and Industry.

[a] Retained imports up to 1969, total imports 1970-7. In the years 1964-71 the differences between retained and total imports were under 0.5 per cent for each main commodity group.

[b] 1936-8 for machinery, transport equipment, textiles and clothing.

[c] SITC groups 711.4-6 are excluded from machinery and included in transport equipment. Certain equipment for continental shelf operations is included in machinery in 1975-7 only.

[d] Including miscellaneous imports, other than gold coins, which are included in the official statistics for 1974-77.

In the first half of the century the development of the internal combustion engine for mass transport and industrial use was accompanied by a spectacular rise in fuel imports and during the twenty years up to 1973 the annual rate of increase still averaged about 7 per cent. But after the huge rises in oil prices in late 1973 the volume of fuel imports fell by nearly a quarter in two years and the development of North Sea oil production reduced imports by about another 25 per cent in 1978.

The volume of imports of manufactures regained its prewar level in five years after the First World War, but the same process took ten years after the Second World War. Subsequently, however, there has been a spectacular rise, most notably in imports of finished goods. Between 1957 and 1977 total imports of finished manufactures increased over twelvefold in volume and, within this group, transport equipment grew nearly seventeenfold. In value terms, the share of machinery and transport equipment was over three times as large a proportion of total imports in 1976-7 as it had been in the late 1950s, while over the same period chemicals and textiles nearly doubled their shares.

In considering the recent growth in imports of manufactures it is important to remember that, whereas their volume is estimated to have increased about two and a half times from 1913 to 1959 for all industrial countries, there was little change in the corresponding figures for the United Kingdom. Over this period the import content of supplies of manufactured goods in the United Kingdom decreased from 17 per cent to 6 per cent and it is estimated that in 1959 imports of manufactures per head of population were about 10 per cent lower than in 1899 and a third lower than in 1913 and 1929. Consequently it seems reasonable to assume that British imports were abnormally low prior to the strong upsurge which produced a fivefold increase between 1957 and 1976-7 in imports of manufactures per head.[1]

Between 1900 and 1973 the United Kingdom's share of the world export trade in manufactures fell from 33 per cent to 9½ per cent, although the importance of production for export in total United Kingdom output was roughly the same at both dates – about a quarter of GNP. Over the same period dramatic changes occurred in the composition of exports. Among commmodities there was a sustained decline in the share of textiles in total exports of manufactures, and a corresponding increase in sales of chemical products, machinery and transport equipment. Among foreign markets there was a fluctuating balance between Sterling Area and West European customers, the former becoming dominant in the interwar years and the latter gaining in relative importance (Table 6.4).

The spread of industrialization abroad – since the mid-1950s starting with Germany and North America in the late nineteenth century – was the key factor determining these trends in export levels and structure. The reduction in Britain's share of output of manufactures that this implied in itself contributed to the reduction in her share of world trade. But more important was a continuous failure to adapt

---

[1] Estimates in this paragraph are from A. Maizels, *Industrial Growth and World Trade*, Cambridge University Press, 1963.

to the new patterns of competition and comparative advantage thrown up by the general economic growth.

This deterioration took place in two phases, separated in time by the Second World War. The first was characterized by a loss of cost advantages in traditional exports. The early specialization in labour-intensive lines such as coal and cotton became increasingly inappropriate in the 1920s as textile industries developed in Asia and mining expanded in the Netherlands and central Europe. Losses in cost competitiveness in iron and steel production *vis-a-vis* Germany and the United States were another important factor. In part, this reflected genuine productivity differences — the British capital stock was older and the labour force slow to adjust to the new industrial order — but the over-valuation of sterling after the gold standard was readopted in 1925 also contributed to the disparities between the United Kingdom's export prices and those of its competitors. The United Kingdom thus failed to profit from growth in advanced economies and by the 1930s nearly half of its export trade was concentrated on the preferential Sterling Area markets. The adverse terms of trade, and hence lower real incomes, encountered by the primary producing countries in the 1930s thus meant declining markets for British goods.

Table 6.4 *Changes in the area and commodity structure of exports,*[a] *1913-77*

Percentages

	1913	1929	1937	1950	1955	1956-63	1964-71	1972-7
Western Europe	31	27	26	26	27	31	44	51
Sterling Area outside Europe	33	39	43	47	49	39	24	18
North America	10	11	12	11	11	15	16	13
Rest of world	26	23	19	16	13	15	16	18
Machinery and transport equipment	11	9	20	37	37	42	42	40
Chemicals	5	5	6	6	8	8	9	11
Textiles	35	26	24	18	11	7	5	4
Metals and metal manufactures	14	12	13	12	12	13	11	10
Other manufactures	13	26	14	10	12	13	17	18
Total manufactures	*78*	*78*	*77*	*83*	*80*	*83*	*84*	*83*

SOURCES: Department of Trade; London and Cambridge Economic Service, *Key Statistics of the British Economy 1900-70.*
[a] Including re-exports after 1963.

The United Kingdom lost ground in a contracting volume of world trade and the potential direct contribution of exports to GNP growth was much reduced.

In the second, postwar, phase of British export growth, the basis for trade shifted emphatically away from the exchange of manufactures for primary products with the Commonwealth and towards an exchange of manufactured goods with other industrialized countries. There was some further erosion of export shares on the earlier pattern, one notable example being the substitution of Japanese iron and steel in Australian and New Zealand imports during the trade liberalization of the mid-1950s. However, the striking feature of that period was the elevation of exports of engineering products to a role no less dominant than that of textiles at the turn of the century, and this was a position to which the commodity mixes of other leading trading nations also converged. In this new environment, in which competitiveness was generated not so much by cost advantages as by aggressive marketing and willingness to meet ever-changing technical standards, the British share of the fast-expanding world trade in manufactures proved extremely vulnerable. It fell from 19 to 9.4 per cent between 1955 and 1977, and two-fifths of the overall decline in the share of world trade since 1900 thus occurred after 1955.

Attempts to explain this diminishing participation in world trade have revolved around two fundamental structural problems of British industry. First, the suppliers of exportable goods, while successfully maintaining their existing stock of machinery, have failed to invest in new techniques or to diversify into new fast-growing product lines. Secondly, the range of exported goods has become very similar to that entering domestic consumption, so that exports are no longer complementary to but rather are competitive with production for the home market. This has meant that British industries depending on scale economies for cost advantages in trade have suffered in comparison with their EEC or North American competitors because of the slow growth of the British economy as a whole. Moreover, in the pursuit of full employment, domestic demand has often been managed close to or beyond its productive potential; producers have had little capacity available to meet new export contracts, and little profit incentive, given the combination of high domestic inflation and fixed exchange rates during most of the 1960s.

The devaluation of 1967 and the subsequent transition to a floating rate in 1972 removed this last constraint and exports of manufactures have clearly benefited (Table 6.5). They grew in volume terms by 6½ per cent per annum between 1967 and 1977 (2 per cent per annum less than world trade) as against 3 per cent per annum (5 per cent less than world trade) in the period 1960-7.

Table 6.5 *Changes in the volume of exports, 1900-77*

Volume indices, 1961=100[a]

	Manufactures						Non-manu-factures	Total goods
	Machinery[b]	Chemi-cals	Textiles[c]	Metals[d]	Other[c]	Total		
1900	9	12	76	35	26	45	n.a.	48
1913	21	23	91	66	47	70	n.a.	83
1929	28	27	34	68	56	65	n.a.	67
1937	23	26	42	53	47	51	n.a.	54
1950	73	45	173	83	90	82	70	82
1955	82	65	135	86	90	86	85	87
1956-63	96	88	111	98	94	96	96	96
1964-71	131	164	115	118	157	136	28	133
1972-7	187	301	160	147	282	206	191	202

SOURCES: Maizels, *Industrial Growth and World Trade*; Department of Trade; NIESR estimates.

[a]Indices based on 1954, 1961 and 1970, linked through overlapping years 1950-5 and 1961-5.

[b]Includes transport equipment.

[c]For years prior to 1950 clothing is included with textiles, rather than in 'other'.

[d]Includes metal goods.

6. Invisibles

The invisible surplus has fallen in real value since the 1920s and prospects for parts of it are not favourable. Of the three components of the account, property income always in the past provided the major source of funds, services have occasionally been in deficit and only in recent years in surplus on the same scale as property income, while transfers have always been in deficit.

After the First World War, shipping receipts, the traditional source of invisible earnings, fell because freight rates and Britain's share of shipping were lower. But in spite of another large fall after the Second World War, in which the merchant fleet was reduced by a quarter, the balance remained positive until the 1950s, since when it has normally been in deficit or equilibrium. The United Kingdom share of tonnage has continued to fall and freight costs have grown faster on imports than on exports. Deficits are likely to continue because of excess capacity and increasing competition. The surplus on civil aviation has in the past been more than sufficient to balance the shipping deficit. On travel there was a deficit on balance in the earlier years, but there has been a sizeable surplus since 1974, which rose sharply, though probably temporarily, to over £1 billion in 1977. Other private services, principally insurance and banking, have had a continuously increasing surplus. They suffered least after both wars and are less sensitive to conditions in the United Kingdom.

Net property income increased rapidly from 1960, when its money value was about the same as in the 1920s, to 1973 when it levelled off at about £1 billion. After the liquidation of British overseas investment to the amount of over £1 billion in the Second World War, it was still much lower in real terms than it had been in the interwar period. The surplus is now falling rapidly because of the interest payments on public sector borrowing (since 1974) and the returns on increased private investment in the United Kingdom (especially since 1977).

Private transfers have never been large. Government transfers and services are a new postwar deficit item, which rose only slowly after 1962 and fell in the late 1960s. Expenditure on administrative services increased rapidly in the postwar period, faster than the rate of inflation, but there was only slow growth in military spending at current prices. There has been a rise in net transfers since 1972 because of net contributions to the EEC, which will increase substantially in coming years, and, particularly since 1975, increases in aid payments, which had stagnated until 1971.

7. Capital Balance

The reversal of the previous net outflow of capital for private investment is one of the major changes in the United Kingdom balance of payments in the last few years. It has been the result of a very slow growth of investment, particularly portfolio investment, from the United Kingdom (except that financed from loans raised abroad), combined with increasing overseas investment in the United Kingdom, particularly in North Sea oil. The outflows, even in the 1950s, were small in real value compared with those of the 1920s and 1930s. The flows of capital in both directions, however, remain very large compared with those of other countries except the United States.

In contrast to the long-term position, short-term liabilities have normally exceeded assets. The growth of the Euro-dollar market has meant a very rapid rise in recent years in both assets and liabilities (Table 6.6), but the net inflow of short-term capital has increased partly because United Kingdom interest rates have been relatively high.

The preferred form of short-term capital inflows in most of the postwar period was official deposits, particularly those of sterling countries, whose holdings have fluctuated least. These had always existed as both the working balances and the long-term holdings of Sterling Area and other countries, but during the Second World War they increased sharply and were more clearly distinguished from

Table 6.6 *External assets and liabilities, 1962 and 1977*

£ *millions*

	1962	1977
Assets		
Private investment abroad	8,070	26,400
Public sector lending etc.	710	2,400
Banking and commercial claims	2,265	92,820
Reserves	1,540	10,975
Total identified external assets	12,585	132,595
Liabilities		
Overseas investment in private sector	3,165	21,640
Overseas loans to government and investment in public sector	3,806	13,256
Banking and commercial liabilities	2,965	95,180
Other public sector capital	1,189	4,895
Total identified external liabilities	11,125	134,970

SOURCE: *Bank of England Quarterly Bulletin*, June 1975; June 1978.

other British liabilities. At that time most of the sterling reserves were held by India, Pakistan and Ceylon, with smaller amounts held by the colonial territories, and holdings by Australia, New Zealand and South Africa comparable with those of North America and Europe. The official attitude to them seems to have changed from worry in the 1930s about their growing size in relation to United Kingdom reserves; anxiety to prevent their reduction and encourage their increase during the late 1940s when their withdrawal could have increased the deficit on the balance of payments; renewed concern over their size in the 1950s and 1960s when the need for finance was less pressing; to efforts to preserve and increase them again in the 1970s. A return to worry in 1976 led to an offer of medium-term foreign currency bonds as a substitute, but only a small proportion of holdings was converted. During the 1950s the Middle East became an important holder and the balances held by the colonial territories increased, while those of the Asian members of the Commonwealth were reduced. The total increased in the early 1970s because of the trade surpluses of the Overseas Sterling Area, particularly those of the oil-producing countries, but the whole increase was lost in 1975 and 1976. Sterling seems unlikely to regain its reserve currency role, although there was little further change in 1977. Its share in total foreign currency reserves fell from about 50 per cent in 1953 to 8 per cent in 1974 and 2 per cent at the end of 1977.

Sterling balances provided a form of external support for the balance of payments throughout the period, particularly in the 1940s. The need for official assistance in the late 1960s followed the declining importance of this traditional source of finance. Finally, although some public borrowing occurred in the 1960s and it increased in 1971 and 1972, the major increase came in 1973 and 1974. All the traditional forms of government borrowing then rose (except sales of government stocks, perhaps because they are denominated in sterling), but they became much less important than the new method of using foreign banks. This expedient provided the relative freedom from policy constraints on the United Kingdom that the use of sterling balances offered until the 1950s. In 1975, however, these forms of public borrowing fell sharply, and in 1976 and 1977 there was a return to official (IMF) assistance.

In the 1930s, and again in the 1950s and 1960s, the official objective was not merely to balance payments but to increase reserves. They were considered too low because the large volume of capital movements and the short-term liabilities, such as the sterling balances, made necessary some protection against sudden withdrawals that might reduce the reserves to below a working balance. This fear has been reduced by floating currencies, but the level of the floating rate itself depends partly on confidence in the ability of the reserves to sustain a temporary outflow.

Reserves rose immediately after the First World War and more slowly in the late 1920s. They rose rapidly after 1932 to reach a level in 1938 that permitted a large outflow of short-term capital. After the Second World War, except for a peak about 1950, they rose slowly until the early 1960s, when fluctuations began, followed by a sharp fall until 1968. Gold was the major part of the reserves between the wars and as late as 1955 it accounted for 94 per cent; since then foreign exchange has become more important. In 1970 and 1971 gold holdings fell, while foreign exchange reserves increased rapidly. Part of this increase was lost in 1972 and there were further small falls in 1975 and 1976. In 1977 there was an unprecedented rise explained by capital inflows (Table 6.1). In order to maintain a stable exchange rate the reserves were allowed to rise to $21 billion by the end of the year.

Controls on capital movements began as informal consultation, particularly on the timing of foreign issues, in the late 1920s. They may have thus prevevnted temporary difficulties, although they had little net effect. In the 1930s they increased, and they were replaced by full exchange control in the Second World War. After the war control continued, and the use of United Kingdom funds for overseas investment was increasingly restricted to investments which promised immediate returns. The result has been an increase in investment financed from unremitted profits and foreign borrowing. Portfolio investment is limited by the use of a pool of investment currency, preventing any increase financed from the United Kingdom. The controls, which at first applied only to investment outside the Sterling Area, were extended to developed countries within the area 'voluntarily' in 1966 and completely in 1972. Inward investment has also been controlled to ensure that the major part is financed from abroad, not from local borrowing. The ending of the net outflow of private investment has thus been consistent with official policy since the war and particularly since the early 1960s.

Chapter 7

THE MANAGEMENT OF THE BRITISH ECONOMY

1. Objectives

The purpose of management is to alter the course of the economy in order to achieve certain objectives — that is, to improve its performance in some way. During the postwar period there has been some change in the emphasis laid on different policy objectives in Britain. First of all, the experience of the war had convinced politicians — and the electorate — that full employment could be attained; the proposition could not be defended that work could be found for all in time of war but not in time of peace. Already, before the end of the war, the coalition government had committed itself to full employment policies, and the Labour government elected in 1945 accepted the preservation of full employment as its dominant economic objective. Secondly, Britain had emerged from the war with a huge imbalance in its overseas trade; the second main objective was to right this imbalance by raising exports and holding down imports. In those early years not much was heard about economic growth, because the concept was probably rather inapposite in a period of reconstruction; the emphasis was simply on more and more production. The idea of an underlying growth-rate which could be accelerated by economic policy was as yet absent. Finally, in the early postwar years not many policy-makers saw the problem of rising prices as a long-term chronic problem; it was more widely held to be a temporary problem of postwar shortages. In the years up to 1950 there was a much greater fear of a possible post-recovery depression than there was of inflation.

In the 1950s, which was a period of Conservative government, the full employment commitment was maintained. We find the balance of payments objective frequently stated in a rather different way: policy-makers constantly referred to the need to maintain 'the strength of sterling' and to preserve Britain's role as a world banker. Gradually, as the decade wore on, there was a growing realization that the problem of rising prices was not just a temporary or cyclical problem, but a continuing one. The price objective was a much more ambitious one then than now, in that policy-makers were concerned if a rise in prices in any year exceeded 3 per cent.

Towards the end of the 1950s a new concern arose, or at least an old concern was phrased in a different way. As international comparisons of growth-rates became available, it became clear that Britain was a slow-growth country. It gradually became an explicit objective of economic policy to accelerate the rate of economic growth. New instruments were devised and new institutions established to this end (they are discussed in the next section). However, in the mid-1960s this new objective of economic growth came into sharp conflict with the balance of payments objective. It was in fact the latter objective which dominated policy from 1964, not only up to the time of devaluation in 1967, but up to the beginning of 1969.

Towards the end of the period there were further changes in emphasis. From 1966 onwards governments of both persuasions accepted a higher level of unemployment than they would have done before. In Britain, as in other industrial countries, the price objective became less ambitious, as the difficulties of finding any effective means of moderating the price rise became more apparent. And, with the floating of the exchange rate in July 1972, the form of the balance of payments objective changed. Both before devaluation, and indeed after it, the government was concerned to maintain a certain fixed parity for sterling, and the balance of payments objective could be expressed as the defence of the exchange rate. As from July 1972 this ceased to be so; the objective of an adequate balance of payments was still there, of course, but the exchange rate became an instrument of policy rather than an objective in its own right. Finally, in the period following the oil price rise at the end of 1973 and the subsequent world depression, we note an increasing pessimism about the government's ability to combine full employment either with an adequate balance of payments or with reasonable stability of prices.

The bulk of economic policy in this period was indeed concerned with these four objectives − full employment, economic growth, an adequate balance of payments and stable prices. However, this is not an exhaustive list; for example, governments also had regional policies and policies which aimed to redistribute income. The government inherited from the 1930s the concept of depressed areas − rechristened in the postwar period Development Areas. These were areas where unemployment tended to be higher than in the country as a whole, and a long succession of policies − for example, subsidizing employment in the Development Areas and forbidding the building of new factories in areas where the demand for labour was high − were designed to check the centripetal tendencies of British industry. For the redistribution of income or wealth, no government had precise, quantified objectives. Labour governments tended to stress in particular the inequalities in the distribution of wealth, and introduced legislation on both capital gains and capital transfers. Conservative governments tended to stress the need for adequate reward for talent, particularly managerial talent, and the changes which they made in income tax rates and allowances often had this objective in mind.

2. Institutions and Instruments

Institutions in Britain would appear to be well designed for a strong, coherent, centralized, economic policy. Central governments in Britain are not faced with a division of powers, as in the United States, nor with powerful federal states, as in Western Germany; nor do they have the problems of coalition governments, as in the Netherlands or Belgium. Consequently there is nothing in the party system to prevent the elaboration of a coherent economic policy, and the Parliamentary system normally allows governments to pass any legislation required without any great difficulty. There are not many constraints in the Parliamentary or legal fields to hinder policy-makers. Further, the country has had, from early on, a comparatively advanced apparatus of economic statistics; its national accounts, for example, were developed early and are highly detailed, and the government throughout the postwar period has had reasonably high level economic advice from economists well trained in Keynesian modes of thinking. Throughout most of the period economic policy has been highly centralized in the Treasury, and it has generally been true that if the Chancellor of the Exchequer and the Prime Minister together decided on a course of economic policy they were usually able to carry it through. Parliament's contribution to economic policy was relatively small.

There are two qualifications to this general picture, of economic policy being essentially decided by the Prime Minister and the Chancellor of the Exchequer on the advice of the Treasury. At various times the Governor of the Bank of England has been accepted as a third partner, with an independent view. How far this has been true has depended both on the complexion of the government and on the personality of the Governor. Secondly, there was a short period of about three years, from 1964 to 1967, when a new department, which had been set up in 1964, had some significant influence – the Department of Economic Affairs. Indeed it had been set up by the incoming Labour government specifically to provide a countervailing force to that of the Treasury, and in the early years of the Labour government it did succeed to some extent in sponsoring ideas other than those of short-term demand management. However, it was essentially the department which was supposed to bring about the acceleration of economic growth; as it became clearer that the balance of payments difficulties of the country would prevent any such acceleration, its power waned, and it ceased to have any important influence on economic policy well before its actual demise in 1969.

Some generalizations are possible about the instruments of economic policy which have been preferred in Britain; here, too, there have been changes over time. In the early postwar years, the main instruments used were physical controls. Industry's basic raw materials were allocated and there was fairly extensive consumer rationing. Indeed Britain took longer than many other countries to dismantle the full apparatus of physical controls; for example, rationing of butter, cheese, margarine, cooking fats and meat continued until 1954, and of house coal until 1958. Steel allocation continued until 1953 and building licences did not end until 1954. So physical controls were still quite important instruments of policy up to the early 1950s.

Thereafter, more traditional instruments of economic policy took over the dominant role. In general, it is true to say that fiscal instruments have been preferred to monetary instruments — certainly if one restricts the comparison to the traditional monetary instruments of open market operations and interest rate changes. There is each year a major fiscal decision at the time of the regular annual Budget, which is introduced at any time between the middle of March and the middle of April according to the government's convenience. The accepted official mode of thinking about the Budget's role in macroeconomic policy has not changed a great deal in the last thirty years. The purpose is to reduce prospective aggregate demand in the economy if it is considered likely to be excessive, or to increase it if it is likely to be deficient. Chancellors have normally presented their Budgets in these terms, explaining at Budget time whether they consider it necessary to stimulate or restrain the economy. It should be noted that by the time the Budget is presented the expenditure estimates for the coming financial year have normally been settled; the items which are varied in the Budget are on the side of tax or revenue rather than expenditure.

There is thus an annual fiscal 'intervention' in the economy at Budget time. The other main group of interventions in British postwar economic history have been those which have taken place quite often in July or August (a time when sterling tends to be seasonally weak) and have been triggered by a balance of payments crisis which has shown itself in a run on the gold and foreign currency reserves. These interventions have tended to be 'packages', which have often included public expenditure cuts, increases in Bank Rate and changes in indirect taxation. The purpose of these packages of measures has been not so much to make some carefully calculated adjustment to the movement of demand in the home economy, but rather to reassure foreign holders of sterling.

On the tax side, the instruments have changed quite considerably during the postwar period, particularly in the field of indirect taxation. In the early 1960s, for example, it was decided that the economy needed more instruments that could be effectively used between annual Budgets, so the 'regulator' was introduced, by which a large group of indirect taxes can be raised or lowered by anything up to 10 per cent. The 10 per cent, it should be noted, is a percentage of the previous rate: for example, if the regulator is brought into full operation to increase taxes, a 25 per cent purchase tax rate would be raised to a 27.5 per cent rate. Then in 1966 the government introduced the selective employment tax; this was essentially a tax on employment in services and construction, and it included a premium on employment in manufacturing industry. The most recent major change was the introduction of VAT in 1973, to replace both purchase tax and the selective employment tax. In the field of direct taxation, the main changes have been in corporation tax.

The government has at its disposal a very large number of different fiscal instruments — if one includes in this cateogyr not only the various forms of tax, but also all the various forms of subsidy, transfer and benefit. These were the instruments used both for regional policy and, of course, for the redistribution of incomes. By the end of the period, there was a very large number of different types of transfer, benefit and tax, some at national and some at local level, and with a means test applied to some of the benefits. One consequence was that, after the rapid inflation at the end of the period covered in this book, families could find themselves both paying tax and receiving benefit. Another consequence of the means-tested benefits was that some of the low paid found that increases in their gross incomes which took them over the means-test limits could being about an actual drop in their net disposable income.

On the expenditure side there was a change in doctrine — much more than a change in actual practice — in the early 1960s. An influential committee then recommended that government expenditure should be planned ahead on a five-year basis and the committee was highly critical of the use of government expenditure as a short-term conjunctural instrument. It argued that this led to great inefficiency and waste, and that in any case expenditure cuts — or for that matter short-term increases in expenditure — usually took much longer to become effective than the government intended. However, although the government in theory accepted this critique of short-term expenditure adjustments, the practice nevertheless remained common throughout the period. Particularly in the packages of measures, which were essentially designed to impress foreign opinion, it continued to be considered more or less obligatory to include some measures reducing public expenditure. The evidence is that in a number of cases the cuts were not particularly effective; they were perhaps valued more for their pronouncement effect than for the reduction in real demand which they brought about.

Monetary policy in Britian has until recently been secondary to fiscal policy. Certainly in the period up to 1950 the Labour government used it very little; they argued, for example, that since they had direct control of large sectors of investment through the Capital Issues Committee and through building licences, they had no need to use the rate of interest for this purpose. Consequently Bank Rate during this early Labour government was hardly used at all. The Conservative government which followed declared itself to be more interested in the use of monetary policy; however, through the bulk of this period the main concern of the Bank of England — certainly so far as medium-term and long-term rates of interest were concerned — was to keep an orderly market so that there could be smooth management of the national debt. Throughout the period the main weapons of monetary policy were non-traditional ones; over the greater part of the period there was some form of direct control over bank advances and the banks were given directives about the type of business which they should favour — such as exports or import-saving projects — and the types of expenditure which they should discourage — such as personal borrowing, or borrowing for property development or for speculative purposes. The other main instrument which was used in the monetary field was also non-traditional; it was the use of hire purchase controls. The government varied the proportion of the total sum borrowed which had to be put down in cash, and also varied the length of the total period over which the borrower had to repay the full sum. The use of this particular instrument also came under heavy criticism on the grounds that it discriminated heavily against particular consumer goods industries, and indeed served to raise costs and prices in those industries; none the less the government has found it so useful an instrument, particularly in its quick effect on consumers' expenditure, that it has been unable to give it up entirely.

The method of control of the banks — and particularly the direct control of bank advances — led to the rapid growth of secondary money markets during this period; the traditional clearing banks began to lose their share of the total provision of credit. Partly for this reason, towards the end of the period an attempt was made to get rid of the direct controls, and to develop a system by which the control was indirect and in which the banks were free to compete against each other. Further, the practice of regular intervention by the Bank of England to prevent any substantial movements in the medium-term or long-term rates of interest was heavily modified. At the end of the period, therefore, the instrument the government was using to influence the supply of credit was no longer the direct control of bank advances, but the requirement on banks to deposit certain sums with the Bank of England — a requirement which could be appropriately varied.

Through most of the postwar period monetary instruments were essentially adjuncts to fiscal instruments. However, in periods when the government had borrowed from the IMF monetary policy came to the fore. The monetary target favoured by the IMF was DCE — domestic credit expansion; this corresponds to the change in the money stock on its M3 definition plus the balance of payments deficit (defined for this purpose, broadly speaking, as the deficit on current account less net private sector borrowing overseas). In 1976 the government began the practice of stating money supply targets as part of its anti-inflationary strategy. Money supply targets could be taken as, in effect, a threat to deflate the economy and create more unemployment if wage awards became excessive.

There are two other general comments to make on the types of instruments which were used: the first concerns exchange rates, and the second concerns the setting up of new institutions. Throughout most of this period, the exchange rate was an instrument of last resort; in the postwar period up to 1970, it was only used twice. Indeed, during most of the period it could more properly be regarded as an objective of economic policy, rather than as an instrument; certainly from 1964 to 1967 it would be right to say that a very large part of economic policy was directed to the defence of the exchange rate. The situation changed with the move to a floating exchange rate in July 1972; from then on it was open to the government, within limits, to manage the movement of the exchange rate, and so to use it to a limited extent as an instrument of economic policy.

Finally, economic policy is not just concerned with the operation of the traditional policy instruments; economic policy-makers during the postwar period have spent an appreciable part of their time in devising and establishing new institutions of one kind or another. Indeed this was probably increasingly true throughout the postwar period. As the following sections make clear, governments in their anti-inflation policy began during the 1960s to give less prominence to demand management and more prominence to institutional change; so from 1960 onwards the history of anti-inflation policy is quite largely the history of the attempts to devise effective incomes policy institutions. In much the same way, new institutions were also set up in the hope that they would serve to stimulate Britain's rate of economic growth — first, the National Economic Development Council, then the Department of Economic Affairs, with the National Plan and, at much the same time, the Industrial Reorganization Corporation, in an attempt to increase British industrial efficiency by promoting mergers where considered desirable. It is, of course, much more difficult to evaluate the effects of institutional change than it is to evaluate the effects of the operation of some well established instrument of policy; for this reason institutional changes tend sometimes to be omitted from analyses, and indeed from descriptions, of economic policy. They none the less constitute a very important part of the whole.

3. The Use of Policy Instruments

It is perhaps useful to describe first a typical 'policy cycle' in Britain; secondly to describe also some of the policy attempts to break out of this cyclical pattern.

We can begin the description of the policy cycle at the end of a period of stagnation, say, at the end of 1958 or 1962. The trigger for government action is usually that it becomes disturbed about the rising figure for unemployment; it then takes steps to stimulate demand — by removing restrictions on consumer credit (as in 1958), or by tax reductions, or by public expenditure changes. There are, however, a number of time lags before these measures become effective; consequently, it may often appear that the first 'injection' of purchasing power is not working. As a result there may be a slight panic and the government will move to pull out more stops, perhaps with encouragement to nationalized industries or local authorities to accelerate their spending plans.

Eventually the stimulus will take hold; output will begin to risee and, after a lag, unemployment will begin to fall. The first signs of a revival in private investment will appear in manufacturers' declarations of their investment intentions; however, the actual turning point in private investment expenditure is probably some way off.

Within a year the first signs will begin to appear of a worsening in the balance of payments. In the early months when this is happening it may well be that the gold and foreign currency reserves do not fall, since some of the countries with whom we are increasing our trade deficit allow their own reserves to be built up in the form of sterling balances. Then at some point along the road — quite often in the summer, which is usually an unfavourable time of the year for sterling — there is a speculative run against sterling. This, in the fixed exchange rate period, forced the government to take severe deflationary action, which it normally did in the form of a 'package' of measures; this package tended not to be carefully constructed, but rather a hasty collection of measures which, it was hoped, would restore confidence among foreign bankers. So the boom would be brought to an end. There were normally other factors, as well as the imposition of government restraints, which served to slow down the rise in output. Supply side constraints would be beginning to appear, since the economy had moved closer to full capacity working. On the demand side, the peak figure for stockbuilding would probably have been reached, and from then on there would be no further demand stimulus from that source. So it happened on more than one occasion that government restraints were imposed on an economy where the rise in output was already slowing down.

At this point in the policy cycle the period of relative stagnation in output begins; after a time lag unemployment begins to rise. With the very slow rise in output, there is also a slowing down in the rise in the volume of imports. Again after a time lag, the increase in private investment is checked and reversed. The balance of payments gradually moves back into surplus, and the stage is set for the next episode of policy-induced expansion.

4. Attempts to Break the Pattern

The course of postwar economic policy can be seen both as a repetition of the pattern described above, and as a series of attempts to break out of the pattern; these attempts are very briefly described here.

Beginning in the 1960s, a number of new institutional devices were tried in an attempt to raise the underlying growth-rate of the British economy. One of the ideas behind the attempt was that, if a sufficient number of major industrialists could be persuaded that a faster growth-rate was indeed likely, then they would undertake the investment programmes which would make this more rapid growth-rate possible. So the indicative plans contained both in the early work of the National Economic Development Council and in the later work of the Department of Economic Affairs incorporated a significant acceleration of past growth-rates. Another aim of this policy was the increased industrial intervention on the part of the Labour government; the policy comprised both the encouragement of certain mergers through the Industrial Reorganization Corporation, and subsidies and other forms of assistance at the frontiers of technology. These various institutional experiments were unsuccessful in making any radical change in Britain's economic growth-rate and the idea of national planning fell into general disrepute. In the 1970s the National Economic Development Council increasingly turned its attention to an 'industrial strategy' of examining the specific problems of individual industries; the National Enterprise Board, set up under the 1975 Industry Act, apart from its responsibility for various 'lame duck' firms such as British Leyland, is also enjoined to promote industrial efficiency and employment and to invest only in projects which it believes will be profitable.

Also during the 1960s experiments were being made with new institutions to deal with the chronic problem of inflation. The Conservative government came to the conclusion that demand management was an unsuccessful method of dealing with inflationary problems and, towards the end of its period of office, the National Incomes Commission was set up. It had a rather short life; it had few powers and no trade union support; it disappeared with the end of the Conservative government in October 1964.

The second institutional attempt to deal with this problem was that of the Labour government. They initiated their incomes policy with a Statement of Intent, signed by representatives of the TUC, the CBI and the government. The basic principle was that of a 'norm' for wage increases, in line with the expected increase in output. Observance of this norm was, essentially, to be voluntary, but the government also established the National Board for Prices and Incomes, which was empowered to deal with references made to it by the government — both on prices and on incomes. However, it only had powers of delay. The policy proved to be a fairly weak one, and it went through a number of vicissitudes during the Labour government's years. For a while the TUC set up its own vetting committee for wage claims; then — after one of the sterling crises which preoccupied the government in this period — there was a wages and prices freeze for six months from mid-1966. The freeze was followed by a period of 'severe restraint', but here again the only power the government possessed was the power of postponement of a wage award on the recommendation of the National Board for Prices and Incomes. In the final period of incomes policy, a good deal of emphasis was given to productivity agreements as justifiable exceptions from the basic 'norm', and a great many awards were dressed up as productivity agreements. By 1969 the government was coming to the conclusion that the potentialities of incomes policy were more or less exhausted and the focus of attention was shifted to the problem of unofficial strikes. It was decided that it might be a more promising approach to find ways of outlawing unofficial strikes; it was therefore proposed to introduce a bill to reform industrial relations. This was faced with such strong opposition from the TUC and from the Labour Party itself that the government was forced to drop this legislation in exchange for a 'solemn and binding' agreement that the TUC would do something about the problem.

The Conservative government came to power in mid-1970 opposed to any form of formal incomes policy. It abolished the National Board for Prices and Incomes. It also proceeded to attempt to bring the trade unions 'within the framework of the law' by an Industrial Relations Act; at the same time it was careful to avoid any vigorous reflationary action to bring unemployment down, and in the public sector it pursued a policy which became known as the 'N−1' policy, under which it attempted to ensure that each successive settlement was 1 per cent lower than the previous one. This policy in effect broke up early in 1972. First of all, the government failed to hold unemployment even at the relatively high level it inherited; right through 1971 unemployment rose rapidly to pass the million mark in early 1972, yet it seemed to have little effect in moderating the size of wage awards. Secondly, the policy of bringing down the size of settlements in the public sector was broken by the miners' strike in early 1972, which in effect forced a government capitulation.

In 1972, therefore, the Conservative government changed its strategy, and made another attempt to break out into a sustained period of faster growth. This strategy included an expansionary Budget, to bring down the rate of unemployment and to give a demand stimulus to investment; it also included a move to a floating exchange rate in mid-1972, in the hope that this would effectively remove the balance of payments constraint on economic growth; the third element in the strategy was the determination to reintroduce some kind of incomes policy. The government attempted in the middle of 1972 to reach a consensus agreement with the trade union leaders, but failed; and in November it adopted a statutory prices and incomes policy. The intention of this combination of policies was to bring about a 5 per cent growth-rate, which the government hoped might persist, combined with a moderate price rise and a balance of payments outcome, which would, as it were, be protected by the falling exchange rate.

This combination of policies did not bring the hoped-for break-through into longer-term faster growth. It is true that in the short term the rise in national output did accelerate during 1972 and early 1973, and in its first and second stages the new statutory incomes policy survived the opposition of the trade union movement. However, although the exchange rate fell, a very substantial balance of payments deficit emerged, which showed no signs of disappearing. This was partly because this particular 'dash for growth' unfortunately coincided with a world commodity price boom, culminating in the trebling of oil prices over the winter of 1973-4. By the middle of 1974 total import prices (in sterling terms) had doubled from their level in 1972.

Finally, the third stage of the Conservative government's incomes policy encountered a miners' strike in the early months of 1974; a general election was called, the Conservative Party failed to get a majority and was succeeded by a Labour government. It is hard to assess as yet how far the Conservative government's strategy was essentially misguided, or how far its failure to accelerate the underlying growth-rate was due to an unfortunate set of international circumstances.

The Labour government came into power in February 1974 at the beginning of a world recession. It abandoned the statutory approach to incomes policy; however, throughout 1974 the provisions of the Conservative government's Stage III policy were still serving to accelerate the rise in wage rates. For this policy, conceived before the increase in oil prices at the end of 1973, provided for full compensation in wage rates for any increase in prices which exceeded 7 per cent from the base date in October 1973. By April 1974 this threshold had been passed, and this provision of the Conservative government's incomes policy continued to push up both wages and prices throughout 1974.

The Labour government's approach to incomes policy was to persuade the trade unions to subscribe to a loosely worded declaration that they intended to be moderate in their wage demands − a declaration called the 'social contract'. The provisions were so imprecise, however, that by the middle of 1975 average earnings were some 28 per cent, and retail prices some 25 per cent, higher than a year earlier. While the rate of inflation was moving rapidly up in this way, national output was falling and unemployment was rising sharply.

In July 1975 there began a series of incomes policies. In the first of these everyone was limited uniformly to an increase of £6 a week; the second (beginning in July 1976) was almost as uniform − £2.50 a week for those earning up to £50 a week, 5 per cent for those earning £50 to £80 a week and £4 a week for all with higher earnings. Both these policies had the support of the trade union movement and by July 1977 the annual increase in average earnings was down to 8 per cent. The third stage of incomes policy had a 'norm' of 10 per cent − this time without official TUC endorsement; the rise in average earnings went up to 14 per cent. In the fourth stage, beginning in July 1978, the government put forwards a 5 per cent 'norm', which met considerable trade union opposition and by the end of the year it was clear that the increase would be considerably higher.

5. Conclusion

It is generally accepted that the performance of the British economy in the last two decades − compared with the performance of other industrial countries in Western Europe − has been poor. The attempt to accelerate the growth-rate from about 3 to 4 per cent failed. Britain's share in world trade in manufactured goods fell in every year from 1950 to 1973, with only one exception (1971); at the beginning of the period this share was 25 per cent; by 1973 it was down to 9½ per cent. Consumer prices rose rather faster, if anything, than the average for other industrial countries, and Britain's record of unemployment was no better than average.

By their own criteria, therefore, economic policy-makers in Britain were unsuccessful; they were wrong in thinking that the particular methods they chose would be powerful enough to transform the situation. It became clear by the early 1960s that the simple manipulation of demand was not adequate to deal with a wage-driven inflation; small increases in unemployment did not lead to a reduced rate of increase in money earnings.

It also became clear that there was no easy technique for manipulating demand so that full employment and an adequate balance of payments could be combined. The problem with using the exchange rate for this purpose is that of retaining the competitive advantage — that is, of preventing the rise in import prices triggering off such an acceleration in the rise in earnings that the advantage is rapidly lost.

INDEX

This book is to be returned on or before
the last date stamped below.

22 DEC 1980

19 NOV 1981

1 1 MAR 1986